EXPLORING THE SUNDAY LECTIONARY

A Teenager's Guide to the Readings
Cycle B

Sandy Rigsby and Steve Mason

Paulist Press
New York/Mahwah, N.J.

NIHIL OBSTAT
Monsignor John P. Zenz, Censor Deputatus

IMPRIMATUR
+ Adam Cardinal Maida, Archbishop of Detroit

October 26, 2004

The Nihil Obstat and Imprimatur are official declarations that a book or pamphlet is free of doctrinal or moral error. No implication is contained therein that those who have granted the Nihil Obstat and the Imprimatur agree with the content, opinions or statements expressed.

Extracts from the Documents of the Second Vatican Council are from Walter Abbot's edition of *The Documents of Vatican II* © 1966 by America Press used by kind permission of America Press. Visit: *www.americamagazine.org.*

Cover design by Rini Twait
Book design by BookComp, Inc.

Library of Congress Cataloging-in-Publication Data

Rigsby, Sandy, 1960–
    Exploring the Sunday lectionary : a teenager's guide to the readings, cycle B / Sandy Rigsby and Steve Mason.
      p. cm.
    ISBN 0-8091-9581-X (alk. paper)
    1. Church year meditations.   2. Bible—Meditations.   3. Teenagers—Religious life.   I. Mason, Steve, 1960 May 15–   II. Title.
    BV30.R54   2005
    242'.63—dc22

                               2005001956

Published by Paulist Press
997 Macarthur Boulevard
Mahwah, New Jersey 07430

www.paulistpress.com

Printed and bound in the
United States of America

Contents

Acknowledgments

This work has been supported by many wonderful people, each of whom has contributed in an important way:

Kevin Carrizo di Camillo has provided excellent guidance and sage advice as editor.

We have also been blessed with a myriad of insightful readers who have given generously of their time and talent to make this work better. To these folks, we owe a debt of gratitude:

Sr. Lauren Cole, RSM
Dennis J. Courtney, Jr.
Joyce Francois
Dr. Frank Lucido
Monica T. Majcher
Fr. William Murphy
Most Reverend Walter Schoenherr
Christopher A. Simon
Fr. Paul Ward
Monsignor John Zenz

Many teens have participated in small group discussions with this material. We thank them for their candid feedback and participation, which has been especially valuable in developing this work.

Finally, we would like to acknowledge our families who have supported us throughout the long hours of writing.

Introduction

"Ignorance of the Scriptures is ignorance of Christ"

Something wonderful happens when young people come together to share their faith through Scripture study. The dynamics of the exercise speaks to a spiritual desire that we all share. Teens especially need to discover for themselves the spiritual wealth of the Scriptures and have an opportunity to articulate their insights in a small community. In this environment spiritual development is nurtured.

Vatican II discusses the importance of Scripture study in its *Dogmatic Constitution on Divine Revelation*:

> This sacred Synod earnestly and specifically urges all the Christian faithful, too, especially religious, to learn by frequent reading of the divine Scriptures the "excelling knowledge of Jesus Christ" (Phil 3:8). "For ignorance of the Scriptures is ignorance of Christ." Therefore, they should gladly put themselves in touch with the sacred text itself, whether it be through the liturgy, rich in the divine word, or through devotional reading, or through instructions suitable for the purpose and other aids which, in our time, are commendably available everywhere, thanks to the approval and active support of the shepherds of the Church. (25)

This book is the culmination of many years of guided Scripture study with young people. The techniques used to lead small group reflection have been refined and proven with teens in various settings from catechetical classes to youth groups to days of recollection. The sessions presented here make a perfect Rite of Christian Initiation for Adults (RCIA) companion and have application in virtually any setting where youth may come together to explore spirituality. Since the format is also excellent for individual personal reflection on the Sunday readings, many people may find this to be an appropriate confirmation, graduation, birthday, or Christmas gift to support the spiritual growth of a special teenager. Most appreciated is the ease with which participants can use this material. A Bible or Sunday Missal is needed; however, no other preparation is required. In a time when teens and catechists are increasingly busier, this resource provides the opportunity for a meaningful reflection on the Sunday readings without an extensive commitment of time.

The heart of this approach is to let participants explore the Scriptures in their own words through carefully guided questioning. Challenging the teens to pay particular attention to the text invites them to understand Scripture more profoundly. Some questions are designed to bridge the scriptural situation or message to experiences in the participant's life. This technique helps young people discover the relevance of Scripture in their own lives. Other questions are designed to engage their feelings and let the teens understand Scripture as events that touched *real* people in various ways. The *Taking My Scripture Home* section provides questions the participants can reflect on in silence without sharing aloud. This fosters personal reflection and helps teens to focus on living consistently with their faith.

Ultimately the objective of this book is to bring teens closer to God through careful reading and reflection on the Sunday readings. It has been said that true wisdom is in knowing which questions to ask. It is our goal to help young Catholics uncover some of the wealth of wisdom stored in Scripture and to foster a better understanding of the Sunday readings and our Catholic faith. This, in turn, will promote a lasting desire to continue the religious formation of youth into their adult years.

First Sunday of Advent

ISAIAH 63:16b–17, 19b; 64:2–7

In biblical times, prophets were not those who could predict future events. Rather, they were called by God to deliver God's messages to the people. The book of Isaiah, written sometime between 750 BC and 500 BC, is divided into three sections and is believed to be the work of three different authors. The first section of this book is attributed to the prophet Isaiah, while the other two sections are believed to be the work of prophets who were followers of Isaiah. This section of the book is a prayer of sorrow.

- In this reading the author speaks of the Lord as Redeemer. What is a redeemer?
- How does one stray from God's ways?
- What does it mean to have a hardened heart?
- Give some examples of how people today have hardened hearts.
- The author wishes that God would leave the heavens to come to Earth. How can people today invite God to stay close to them?
- What are some awesome deeds that God has done that we can recognize today?
- The author uses the image of God being a potter and people being clay. What do you think this image suggests about the relationship between God and people?
- What other modern-day images would make the same statement?

Taking My Scripture Home

What can you do daily to avoid developing a hardened heart? How can you recognize God's awesome deeds every day?

RESPONSORIAL PSALM REFLECTION: PSALM 80:4

- What does it mean to turn to God?
- How can you see God in your daily life?

1 CORINTHIANS 1:3–9

St. Paul wrote this letter to the church of Corinth around AD 56. This letter teaches the people of Corinth about moral issues, problems in the church, treatment of each other, and basic guidelines for being a Christian. This section of the letter is the greeting to the church of Corinth.

- St. Paul begins the greeting with the words *Grace to you.* What is grace?
- St. Paul goes on to give thanks. What is St. Paul thankful for in this greeting?
- Why is St. Paul thankful?
- What is a spiritual gift?
- Who are some people that you know who have spiritual gifts?
- How do you think St. Paul felt about the church of Corinth?
- In this greeting what did St. Paul say to encourage the Corinthians?
- How do people encourage each other today?

Taking my Scripture Home

Who are the people for whom you are thankful? Why are you thankful for them? How can you remember to encourage those who need support?

MARK 13:33–37

The Gospel of Mark is believed to be the first Gospel and was written around AD 70. St. Mark wrote this Gospel for the Christians in Rome shortly after their violent persecution at the hands of Nero. In this passage Jesus speaks to his disciples of the need to stay awake and be alert.

- Why do you think it is necessary to stay alert and awake?
- What should we look for?
- In this passage Jesus speaks of a man traveling abroad and the gatekeeper keeping watch. Who do you think the man represents?
- Who do you suppose the gatekeeper represents?
- What are some ways you can prepare yourself to meet God?
- Jesus says that the master of the house will come unannounced. How could you possibly be faced with an unexpected opportunity to meet God?
- Do you believe God is present right now in our everyday life, or do we have to wait to meet God? Explain.

- Do you suppose most people anticipate meeting God at the time they die, or do most people look to find God in their everyday lives?
- What are some ways we miss or overlook God's presence in the world around us?
- What can you do to prepare yourself to find God in your everyday life?

Taking My Scripture Home

Where do you find God's presence? Where do you have a difficult time seeing God's presence in your daily life? How would remembering God's constant presence change your daily life?

Second Sunday of Advent

ISAIAH 40:1–5, 9–11

This reading comes from the second section of the book of Isaiah and was probably written by a follower of the original Isaiah. This section is believed to have been written during the Babylonian exile while the Israelites were being held captive. Here the author offers comfort and hope to the Israelites.

- The prophet speaks of a voice crying in the wilderness. Why would this be a welcome sign to someone who was being held captive?
- Why do you think the author used the image of valleys rising, mountains lowering, and level ground?
- Why is it easier to walk on ground that is level?
- What are some difficult things that people your age sometimes have to endure?
- The prophet describes God as a shepherd. What specifically does a shepherd do?
- In what ways would a shepherd protect his or her sheep?
- How would a shepherd comfort his or her sheep?
- Why do you think the prophet used this image to describe God?

Taking My Scripture Home

How do you imagine God to be? How can imagining God as a shepherd be comforting when you are going through difficult times?

RESPONSORIAL PSALM REFLECTION: PSALM 85:8

- Where do you see God's kindness in your everyday life?
- What does salvation mean?
- How do we receive salvation?

2 PETER 3:8–14

The second letter of Peter is believed to have been written around AD 130 by one of St. Peter's followers. In this passage the author is encouraging those who were becoming impatient for Christ's return. The author emphasizes the need to maintain a pure heart while awaiting Jesus.

- The author encourages the audience to be patient and reminds them that God's timetable is different than ours. What are some ways people are impatient with God today?
- If you could control the timing of events, what would you change?
- Describe the chaos that could happen if people were in control of events and time.
- The author instructs the audience to be holy and faithful. What do you suppose this means?
- How can people live holy and faithful lives today?
- What daily choices can people your age make to be holy and faithful?
- The author encourages the audience to be at peace. How can leading a holy and faithful life lead to peace?
- How can impatience lead to frustration instead of peace?

Taking My Scripture Home

What does leading a holy and faithful life mean to you? What choices can you make each day to become more holy and faithful? How can you promote peace in your life?

MARK 1:1–8

In Advent we look forward to the second coming of Christ—his coming in glory—by remembering his first coming. This reading is taken from the beginning of Mark's Gospel to remind us how John the Baptist went about preparing the people for the first coming of Jesus.

- The author begins this book by quoting Scripture from Isaiah. In what ways would John the Baptist's voice or message be a welcome sign to people?
- John the Baptist announced repentance for the forgiveness of sin. What does it mean to repent?
- How can repentance lead to forgiveness?
- How is John the Baptist described in this passage?
- What can we do to prepare ourselves to receive Jesus' teachings?
- John the Baptist did all he could do to point the way to Jesus. What are some ways we can point others to God through our actions and attitudes?
- This passage speaks of John baptizing people with water. Why do you suppose it is important for us to cleanse our attitudes and hearts in order to more fully receive God's Word?

- What are some ways we can purify our intentions?
- What do you suppose John meant when he said Jesus would baptize with the Holy Spirit?

Taking My Scripture Home

John the Baptist talked about the need to repent and be forgiven. Is there a place in your life where you need forgiveness? What can you do to express your desire to be closer to God?

Third Sunday of Advent

The tone of Advent becomes more joyful on this Sunday. Notice the liturgical color changes to rose and how the readings reflect a more joyful tone.

ISAIAH 61:1–2a, 10–11

This passage comes from the third section of the book of Isaiah and is believed to have been written by a follower of the original Isaiah. Luke 4:16–21 tells the story of Jesus reading the first two verses of this passage in the synagogue. Jesus then explains that this text is coming to fulfillment in him.

- The prophet speaks of his mission as carrying out wonderful deeds. What are some of those deeds?
- What does the word *anointed* mean?
- Have you ever been anointed? When or where?
- How do you see your mission as a Catholic Christian?
- What are ways in today's society that you can give good news to the poor or help someone who is sad?
- What other ways can you bring God's love to people?
- In the second part of this reading the prophet speaks of happiness and joy in the Lord. How can helping others make us joyful?

Taking My Scripture Home

What are some ways you follow your mission as a Catholic Christian each day? How can you follow the mission to bring God's love to all people more faithfully each day?

RESPONSORIAL PSALM REFLECTION: ISAIAH 61:10b

- Do you truly rejoice in God?
- What are the characteristics of one who truly rejoices in God?

1 THESSALONIANS 5:16–24

The first letter of St. Paul to the people of Thessalonica is one of the oldest books in the New Testament. It is believed to have been written around AD 50. St. Paul had spent time in Thessalonica and began a church in the city. In this passage St. Paul encourages the Thessalonians to be open to the Spirit. He concludes his letter with a prayer.

- What are the three things St. Paul encourages in the first three verses?
- Why do you think these actions are important to living a Christian life?
- How does someone pray without stopping?
- What exactly qualifies as a prayer?
- Where are some places that someone could pray?
- What does it mean to not quench the Spirit?
- What is the difference between going through the motions of a formal prayer and praying from your heart?
- What are some examples of times when it is difficult to give thanks?
- Can you be thankful in all situations? Explain.

Taking My Scripture Home

When is it most difficult for you to give thanks to God? How can you remember to be thankful and grateful during those times? How can you develop the habit of praying throughout the day?

JOHN 1:6–8, 19–28

Matthew, Mark, and Luke are called "Synoptic" Gospels; they give a similar eyewitness description of Jesus' life. The book of John is different from the other Gospels; it uses symbolic language to describe Jesus and his mission on Earth. This book was written around AD 90. The author is unknown, but was possibly a follower of the Beloved Disciple mentioned in this Gospel.

- The author expresses that John the Baptist came to testify to the light. What or who is the light?
- Why do you suppose light would be a symbol for Jesus?
- In what ways did Jesus bring hope to people?
- The books of Mark and John both quote this verse from Isaiah. Why do you suppose this verse is so important?
- What do you think it means to *make straight the way of the Lord*?
- How do you prepare a way for God each day?
- What are some ways people prepare to receive houseguests?
- Why is it important to prepare ourselves to experience God's presence?
- How would you describe someone who is open and prepared to receive God?

Taking My Scripture Home

How do you testify to the light of Jesus each day? How can you prepare a way for God's love to reach others?

Fourth Sunday of Advent

2 SAMUEL 7:1–5, 8b–12, 14a, 16

The books of Samuel have some of the most wonderful, touching, and meaningful stories found anywhere in the Bible. Both 1 and 2 Samuel tell the story of three key characters: Samuel, Saul, and David. These stories are rich with accounts of how the Lord intervened in their lives and helped them lead the Jewish people. In this passage God looks favorably on his servant David and promises to make him a strong and enduring leader of a great nation. The ark of God is sometimes called the ark of the covenant. It was a sacred box that held the Ten Commandments and was believed to be a place where God lived.

- David expressed to Nathan his concern that the ark of God was in a tent while he enjoyed the comfort of a cedar home. What can you tell about David's attitude and respect for God from his concern?
- What are some ways we can show respect for God's presence?
- In the second part of this reading Nathan delivers a message for David, reminding him of all that the Lord has done for him and all the favor the Lord will bestow on him in the future. Why is it good for us to remember the blessings God has given to us?
- What are some ways God works through people to make their lives better?
- How do you suppose David might have felt when he heard these words from the Lord?
- How do you feel knowing God loves you more than you can love yourself?

Taking My Scripture Home

What are some ways you and your family depend on God? What attitudes or actions represent the natural response of someone who remembers God's goodness? How can you invite such an attitude to dwell inside your heart?

RESPONSORIAL PSALM REFLECTION: PSALM 89:2a

- How does singing the goodness of the Lord help a person remember that she or he depends on God?
- How does singing the goodness of the Lord help a person form a grateful heart?
- What are some ways your actions can sing of the Lord's goodness?

ROMANS 16:25–27

This passage is taken from the very end of the letter of St. Paul to the Romans, which was written around AD 56. St. Paul is referring to how salvation comes to us through faith in response to the revelation of the mystery of Jesus Christ. This was a major theme in his teaching and he is emphasizing it one last time as he concludes this letter.

- St. Paul writes of a mystery that has been kept secret for a long time but that is now revealed by God through Jesus. Why do you suppose salvation through faith was a mystery?
- What is faith?
- How can having faith in God's unconditional love help us when we are going through difficult times?
- What was it about Jesus' teaching and life that made such a difference?
- In Advent we prepare ourselves to celebrate the birth of Christ at Christmas. How do these words of St. Paul help us appreciate the significance of Christ's birth?

Taking My Scripture Home

What can you do these next few days to prepare yourself to celebrate Christ's birth? How can you deepen your faith in God's love during the Christmas season?

LUKE 1:26–38

This announcement to Mary is reminiscent of the message the Lord spoke to David in the first reading. In the first reading God announced that David's heir will be a son of God and that God's kingdom will endure forever. In this reading the theme is taken up again as the angel Gabriel announces that Mary's son will be given the throne of David, he will be called the Son of God, and his kingdom will have no end.

- What are the similarities between Gabriel's description of Mary's son and the message from God in the first reading regarding the heir of David?
- When the angel Gabriel greeted Mary, she was troubled and afraid. Why do you suppose she felt that way?

- After hearing Gabriel's explanation of what was going to happen, how did Mary respond?
- What does Mary's response to Gabriel say about her faith and trust in God?
- What are some opportunities we have to open our hearts to God's presence?
- As the woman who gave birth to Jesus, Mary has a special place in the history of our Church. What are some ways we can give birth to God's love and forgiveness in our families and in our communities?
- During Advent we prepare our hearts to be more responsive to God's presence. What are some ways we can imitate Mary's example in this story?
- Who are some people you know who are open to letting God work through them?
- What do you admire most about these people?

Taking My Scripture Home

Mary listened to Gabriel's message and opened her heart to God's will. What can you do this week to listen more closely to God's Word? How can your actions reveal that you are willing to let God's Word have more control over your life?

The Nativity of the Lord

December 25
Mass During the Day

ISAIAH 52:7–10

This passage from Isaiah is set in a time when the Jewish people were exiled in Babylon. The author is anticipating the joy of Israel on their release and praise for God who set them free. The words used to describe this experience in Israel's history are fitting to celebrate the significance of Jesus' birth for all humanity.

- How would you describe the tone of this passage?
- The author in this passage was anticipating the release of the Jewish people from exile. How can selfishness, greed, or insecurities cause us to be exiled or separated from God?
- What are some ways Christ's message of love, truth, forgiveness, and humility frees us from the slavery of our sin?
- In your own words how would you describe the way the author feels about God in this passage?
- What are some ways the Lord comforts people today?

Taking My Scripture Home

What can you do to ensure that selfishness, greed, or insecurities do not come between you and God? How can you celebrate the fact that God's love has touched your life?

RESPONSORIAL PSALM REFLECTION: PSALM 98:3c

- What sort of power does love and forgiveness have over people?
- What are some ways you have seen God's saving power in your life?

HEBREWS 1:1–6

The book of Hebrews serves as an encouragement to follow Christ more closely. This passage, taken from the beginning of Hebrews, sets the tone by reflecting on the significance of Christ in history and how Jesus is truly the Son of God, greater even than the angels. This was an important distinction, for it was believed that angels acted as arbitrators of the old covenant. By establishing that Jesus was superior to the angels, the author shows that the new covenant is superior to the old.

- The author writes of how God spoke in *incomplete ways* through the prophets. What do you suppose this means?
- By contrast the author says that God has now spoken through Jesus. How is the life of Jesus a more complete form of communication from God?
- Some people tell you how you should act and others show through example the right way to act. How did Jesus do both?
- Why do you suppose it is important for the author to establish that Jesus is superior to the angels?
- How does Jesus' teachings of turning the other cheek and forgiving people seven times seventy times go beyond the laws of the old covenant?
- This passage speaks of the angels worshiping Jesus. How can people worship God through their attitudes and actions?
- Why is it important to act with reverence and respect toward Jesus?

Taking My Scripture Home

To worship God there must first be reverence and respect. What can you do to open your heart to the wonder and awe of God's presence? How can your actions reveal that you respect all of God's creation?

JOHN 1:1–18

The theme introduced here in the prologue, Jesus as the Word of God, recurs throughout John's Gospel. John places special emphasis on Jesus as the Word of God who became flesh and came to live among us. John points out the significance of Jesus as existing eternally with God the Creator and the magnificent event of having that Word become human and live among us.

- What significance does light have in our culture today?
- Why do you suppose John refers to Jesus as the true light of the world that overcomes darkness?
- John mentions how Jesus gave the power to be children of God to those who accepted him. What does it mean to become a child of God?
- Later in this passage John writes how Moses gave the law but that Jesus gave us grace and truth. What is this grace and truth that Jesus gave?

- Why do you suppose it is important to contrast the difference between Moses' laws and Jesus' grace?
- How can our actions and attitudes continue to be a light in the world?
- John mentions that no one has ever seen God. Have you ever seen God's love at work in someone? Explain.

Taking My Scripture Home

What can you do this week to be a light to other people? Who are some of the people that have been a light in your life? How can you show your gratitude to these people for being an example of God's love?

The Holy Family

SIRACH 3:2–7, 12–14

The book of Sirach was written by Ben Sira around 200–175 BC and translated from Hebrew by his grandson after 132 BC. While this book is not included in most Protestant Bibles, it is included in the Catholic canon. This book is designed to provide moral guidance about a variety of topics. In this passage Ben Sira speaks of the virtues that come to those who treat their parents with respect.

- This passage speaks of the importance of honoring and revering one's parents. What does it mean to honor or revere someone?
- Why do you suppose honoring your parents is important?
- How do respect and obedience help keep a family strong?
- Why do you suppose relationships suffer when we take each other for granted?
- The author writes how kindness to a father will not be forgotten. What are some ways kindness toward others brings blessings to a person?

Taking My Scripture Home

What are some ways you can honor your parents? How can you show respect to those in authority?

RESPONSORIAL PSALM REFLECTION: PSALM 128:1

- What does it mean to fear the Lord?
- How does one walk in the ways of the Lord?
- What are some blessings that come to a person whose heart is filled with respect?

COLOSSIANS 3:12–21

It is believed that St. Paul wrote the letter to the Colossians, although it may have been written by one of his followers. The church at Colossae questioned the divine authority and power of Jesus, and this brief letter attempts to establish that faith in Christ is necessary for salvation. In this passage the author is urging the Colossians to love one another and act in ways that build up each other and the community.

- How do attitudes such as humility, compassion, and gentleness help build up a community?
- How do you feel when someone treats you with compassion or kindness?
- The author speaks of how love is the bond of perfection. What do you suppose this means?
- How do we let the peace of Christ control our hearts?
- Why is it important for us to be thankful?
- How can you tell if someone has a grateful heart?
- Why do you suppose obeying your parents is pleasing to the Lord?
- If you were giving advice to someone, what would you say is the most important thing a person can do to build a strong family?

Taking My Scripture Home

What are some qualities you are grateful for in members of your family? What can you do to show your gratitude to your parents, brothers, and sisters? What can you do to extend God's love beyond your family?

LUKE 2:22–40

Mary and Joseph were devout Jews trying to fulfill the law of the Lord by bringing Jesus to the temple for presentation. The law called for all firstborn sons to be consecrated to the Lord. Both Simeon and Anna speak of Jesus as the fulfillment of their hopes that God's rule would return to Israel.

- What does the word *consecrate* mean?
- It was Jewish custom to consecrate firstborn sons to God. How do we Christians consecrate ourselves to God?
- Simeon was a devout Jew who patiently awaited the Messiah. Why do you suppose his eyes were open to the significance Jesus held for his people?
- What are some ways we can be open to seeing the good in ourselves and in others?
- Anna is described as a very prayerful woman. How do you suppose she felt about Jesus and what he would mean to the people?
- What effect does being prayerful have on a person?
- The things that were said about Jesus amazed Joseph and Mary. Why do you suppose they were so amazed?

- Sometimes it is difficult to see the wonderful qualities of those people we know very well. How can we see the goodness in people we know best?
- How do you feel when someone recognizes the goodness in you?

Taking My Scripture Home

Simeon and Anna were hopeful as they patiently waited for the Messiah. What are some things that you are hopeful will happen in your life? How can prayer and patience help you persevere in your faith?

The Solemnity of the Blessed Virgin Mary, Mother of God

January 1

NUMBERS 6:22–27

This passage is a blessing that God gave to the Israelites. It is still used as a doxology, or prayer of praise to God, in many churches today.

- What is a blessing?
- How do you suppose Moses and Aaron felt when God gave them this blessing?
- How does this blessing show God's love and concern for people?
- What can we learn about God from this blessing?
- How can you be a blessing to the people you meet?

Taking My Scripture Home

How can you use this blessing daily to remind yourself of God's love and concern for you? How can this blessing be a comfort to you?

RESPONSORIAL PSALM REFLECTION: PSALM 67:2a

- What does the word *mercy* mean?
- How does God bless us with mercy?
- What are some ways we can bless others with mercy?

GALATIANS 4:4–7

The letter of St. Paul to the church in Galatia was written around AD 55. Having recently converted from pagan religions to Christianity, the Galatians were being disturbed by "Judaizers," those who said that gospel faith needed to be completed by Jewish ritual observances. St. Paul explained emphatically that such Jewish customs were no longer necessary; baptism had replaced circumcision and made them children of God, members of the covenant people.

- St. Paul mentions that God sent Jesus in the *fullness of time*. What do you suppose this means?
- Do you think God's timeline is different from ours? Why or why not?
- What is the difference between a slave and a son?
- In St. Paul's time how significant was the difference between a slave and a son?
- What is the difference between the way a slave treats a master and a son treats a father?
- St. Paul mentions that God sent the Spirit of Jesus into our hearts. What does this mean?
- How would you know if you met someone who had God's Spirit dwelling within him or her?

Taking My Scripture Home

What does it mean in your daily life to treat God as a loving father? How can knowing that God loves you as a loving father enrich your attitude about being a Catholic Christian?

LUKE 2:16–21

The book of Luke was written by a non-Jewish (Gentile) man named Luke. It was written around AD 80 and shows Jesus as a compassionate, forgiving Messiah. In this Gospel Luke portrays Jesus as especially attentive to the poor, meek, and needy.

- Luke tells the story of the shepherds visiting Mary, Joseph, and Jesus. In Jesus' time shepherds were considered unimportant and insignificant. Why do you suppose Luke included this story in his Gospel?
- People listened and believed what the shepherds told them. Why do you think people listened to shepherds of such lowly status?
- How can our enthusiasm about God's love for us be a witness to others?
- The shepherds returned to their work, praising God. What does this say about the mind-set of the shepherds?
- What are some reasons we should praise God for Jesus' birth?
- Mary reflected on all these events. Why is taking time to reflect on events in our own lives important?
- Mary has a special place for Christians as the mother of God. How can her humility and openness to God's will be an example to us?

Taking My Scripture Home

How do you show your enthusiasm for God each day? How can you schedule your day to set aside time for refection on the day's events? Is praise for God a part of your daily life?

Epiphany

ISAIAH 60:1–6

This passage, taken from the last section of Isaiah, was written when the Israelites were being released from exile in Babylon. The author envisions a new Jerusalem that serves as an example to all the nations. Reaching out to the Gentiles (non-Jews) and looking toward the time of Jerusalem's restoration are recurring themes in this final section of Isaiah.

- What do you suppose it means to have the *glory of the Lord shine upon you?*
- The author speaks of how Jerusalem will have a positive effect on other nations. How can nations have a positive effect on each other?
- How can our actions have a positive effect on other people?
- Why do you suppose Jerusalem was favored by God?
- How can nations today act according to God's will?
- How can people act according to God's will?

Taking My Scripture Home

Describe actions that have a positive effect on others. What type of actions have a negative effect? How can you remember to use your actions to share God's love with others?

RESPONSORIAL PSALM REFLECTION: PSALM 72:11

- What does it mean to adore someone?
- Why is God worthy of our adoration?
- Describe a world in which every nation loves God.

EPHESIANS 3:2–3a, 5–6

Ephesians is believed to have been written around AD 80 by one of St. Paul's followers. The mystery the author speaks of in this passage is that salvation is for all people, not just Jews. Many Jewish people at the time had difficulty accepting this idea.

- The author was given a revelation by God. What did the author do with the message?
- Why was sharing this message important at the time?
- In today's society why is sharing the message of God's love important?
- The mystery or revelation was that God loved all people and that all people were a part of God's plan of salvation. Why do you suppose this message still needs to be told?
- Where have you seen prejudices against people or races in today's society?
- The author explains that we are all part of the same body. What do you suppose this means?
- Do you think the words *coheirs* and *copartners* imply equality? Why or why not?

Taking My Scripture Home

How well do you accept people of different races and cultures? What are some ways you can fight discrimination in today's society?

MATTHEW 2:1–12

The Gospel of Matthew was written around AD 85. The author is thought to be Matthew the Apostle. This story is rich with images of following the unknown, trust in God, and honoring Jesus.

- How did the magi know about Jesus' birth?
- How do people today search for God?
- What are some signs of God's presence in today's world?
- What do you suppose was Herod's motive for interviewing the magi?
- How was the news of Jesus' birth a threat to Herod?
- How might Jesus' teaching threaten people today?
- What are some examples of how fear affects the motives of people today?
- How did the magi respond when they found Jesus?
- Why do you think they responded this way?
- What are some ways you have experienced God's presence?
- How does knowing God fill people with joy?

Taking My Scripture Home

In what ways can you become more open to God's presence in the world? What are some ways you can open your heart and share your gifts with others?

The Baptism of the Lord

ISAIAH 42:1–4, 6–7

This passage from Isaiah is one of four "Servant Songs." These passages give a description of the ideal leader, one who serves. It is unclear exactly whom or what the author was referring to by this servant. As Christians, though, we believe Jesus is the one who fulfills this prophecy.

- The author refers to the servant as the one who will bring justice to the nations. What is meant by justice and why is it important?
- The word *justice* often has connotations of punishment. Yet the author speaks of a gentle servant who brings justice without breaking a reed or quenching a smoldering wick. How do these words describe the qualities of Jesus?
- Which is easier, to talk about justice or to live in a way that shows justice? Explain.
- The servant is described as giving sight to the blind and freeing those in dungeons. What are some examples of injustices people suffer in our community today?
- What can be done to challenge these injustices?

Taking My Scripture Home

Do you know anyone who suffers from injustices or cruelty? What can you do to comfort this person? How can you challenge the source of the unjust actions?

RESPONSORIAL PSALM REFLECTION: PSALM 29:11b

- How is peace a blessing?
- How does God's message of love and forgiveness bring about peace?
- Why is it important to experience peace in our hearts?

ACTS 10:34–38

In this reading St. Peter is speaking to a group of Gentiles. At the time the gospel message was thought to be only for the Jewish people, not the Gentiles. St. Peter, in a vision, was told by God to convey the gospel message to Gentiles as well as Jews. This passage is a brief lecture given by St. Peter to Cornelius and his family. This type of teaching was typical in this time.

- St. Peter says that God is impartial, that anyone who fears God and acts uprightly is acceptable in God's eyes. What does it mean to fear the Lord?
- What do fear and respect for the Lord have in common?
- How can you show respect for God and God's creation?
- What are examples of actions and attitudes that are upright?
- How do you feel knowing God's love is available to all people?
- After John baptized Jesus, Jesus began his public ministry. How are we called to imitate Jesus after our baptism?
- St. Peter says that Jesus went about doing good and healing all those oppressed by the devil. What are some ways people your age might need healing?
- How can your words and actions help bring healing to others?

Taking My Scripture Home

To fear God is to respect and hold God in reverence. What is it about God that fills you with awe? What are some ways you can be a healing influence on others?

MARK 1:7–11

Jesus' baptism by John symbolizes his unity with the Jewish people. At the moment of his baptism Jesus is acknowledged as God's own beloved Son. This marks the beginning of his public ministry. Jesus later creates a new people of God by baptizing with the Holy Spirit.

- What happens to a person at baptism?
- Why do you suppose water is used at baptism?
- Why is baptism important to someone who wants to follow Jesus?
- What do you suppose it means to be baptized with the Holy Spirit?
- In this passage a voice from heaven announced favor on Jesus as he came out of the water. What are some ways you feel God's favor in your heart when you live in the purity of your baptism?
- Jesus is described as having the Spirit descend upon him. What are some examples of gifts that come from the Holy Spirit?
- How does the sacrament of confirmation help people live in God's Spirit?
- What are some attitudes and actions you might expect from someone in whom God's Spirit is strong?

Taking My Scripture Home

Baptism purifies our hearts and signifies that we now belong to Christ. What are some ways you can purify your heart every day? How can you open your heart to let God's Spirit work through you more completely?

First Sunday of Lent

GENESIS 9:8–15

Many ancient civilizations had similar stories about floods that destroyed the Earth. In the Genesis version God floods the Earth because of sin and immorality. God saves Noah and his family because of Noah's integrity and establishes a covenant with all living creatures.

- What is a covenant?
- Why did God establish a covenant with Noah?
- In this story why did God flood the Earth?
- In this story Noah did not follow the morals and values of society. In today's society what are some of the morals and values that Christians should not follow?

Taking My Scripture Home

How can you distinguish between society's values and Christian values? What role does peer pressure play in deciding what is morally correct? How can you strengthen yourself to withstand all forms of peer pressure?

RESPONSORIAL PSALM REFLECTION: PSALM 25:10

- What are God's ways?
- How can one keep God's covenant?

1 PETER 3:18–22

St. Peter or one of his disciples wrote this letter sometime between AD 60 and 90 to a community that was being persecuted for their Christian values and beliefs. The author maintains that the waters of the flood foreshadow the saving waters of baptism.

- Why did Christ suffer?
- How can Christ's death and resurrection lead us to God?
- How does baptism save us?
- Why is it important to have a clear conscience?
- What happens to people when they have a guilty conscience?

Taking My Scripture Home

When do you feel as if your soul could use a bath? What can you do to help cleanse your soul and clear your conscience? How does God's forgiveness help clear your conscience?

MARK 1:12–15

The temptation of Jesus in the desert is found in all three Synoptic Gospels and one of the three accounts is always read on the First Sunday of Lent. Mark's account is the shortest, emphasizing through its symbolism that Jesus' conquering of temptation foreshadows a new creation.

- Describe what happened to Jesus in the desert.
- What are some temptations people face in society today?
- What are some temptations that people your age face every day at school?
- What are some ways to resist temptation?
- How can resisting temptation strengthen someone's principles or beliefs?
- Why do you think the Spirit sent Jesus into the desert?
- Jesus began his ministry by telling people to repent. What does it mean to repent?
- What is the difference between believing in the gospel and just hearing the gospel?

Taking My Scripture Home

Do you believe in the gospel? How can believing in the gospel help strengthen you against all temptation? How do your attitudes toward others show that you believe in the gospel?

Second Sunday of Lent

GENESIS 22:1–2, 9a, 10–13, 15–18

The stories in Genesis were passed down by oral tradition. In this story Abraham's obedience and faith in God are tested. Despite his love for his son Isaac, Abraham shows that his love of God and obedience to God are most important in his life. These priorities are richly rewarded, as God blesses Abraham with countless descendents.

- How would retelling stories of faith have been beneficial to the Jewish people?
- Do you think keeping track of stories using only spoken words would work today? Explain.
- In this story Abraham loved his son Isaac very much. How do you suppose Abraham felt when he was told to sacrifice Isaac?
- What are some things in today's society that people might be reluctant to sacrifice for God?
- Why do you suppose it is important to be obedient to God?
- What does this story say about Abraham's values and priorities?
- What are examples of how people today can arrange their priorities in a way that shows respect and obedience for God?

Taking My Scripture Home

God tested Abraham by asking him to sacrifice his beloved son. What are the things in your life that you would find very difficult to sacrifice for God? How can you deepen your dependence upon God?

RESPONSORIAL PSALM REFLECTION: PSALM 116:9

- What does it mean to *walk before the Lord?*
- How would you describe *the land of the living?*
- How does our dependence upon God bring blessings into our lives?

ROMANS 8:31b–34

The people in the church of Rome faced much opposition to their Christian values and beliefs. There was not only conflict with the Jewish leaders, but many Christians faced rejection from their own families. In this passage St. Paul encourages the Romans to take heart against those who might condemn them for their life in Christ.

- St. Paul begins this passage saying God is for us. What does it mean to say *God is for us?*
- Who is the *us* that St. Paul is referring to?
- Name some characteristics of God as described in this passage.
- St. Paul says that Jesus is at the right hand of God and intercedes for us. What do you suppose this means for those who are open to living in God's love?
- How can peer pressure and marketing messages cause people to feel unworthy or inadequate?
- How can our knowledge that God is for us help us handle society's pressures?
- St. Paul speaks of God's generosity and faithfulness to us. How can this passage help us become more secure in our faith?
- What does it mean to be secure in your faith?

Taking My Scripture Home

Where in your life do you question your own goodness or worth? How can you let St. Paul's message that you are forgiven and God is for you help you deal with these feelings?

MARK 9:2–10

The transfiguration of Jesus was a sign to help the disciples understand that Jesus shared in the glory of God. Moses represented the law and Elijah represented the prophets. Their presence on Mount Sinai with Jesus symbolically showed that Jesus was about to fulfill the law and prophecy with his death and resurrection.

- The significance of Jesus' death and resurrection must have been difficult for the disciples to appreciate before his death. How do you suppose this sign helped the disciples understand who Jesus was?

- Do you suppose this episode had more meaning for the disciples *after* Jesus rose from the dead? Explain.
- Today some people do not have proper reverence or appreciation for the significance of God's presence in their lives. Why do you suppose some people struggle to appreciate God's presence?
- What are some miracles that we see every day that show us God's glory?
- What are some ways we can deepen our appreciation and reverence for God?
- In this passage the voice instructed the disciples to listen to Jesus, his beloved Son. Where do we hear God's voice in our lives?
- How can listening to and taking to heart Jesus' message transfigure our attitudes and lives?

Taking My Scripture Home

How can your actions and attitudes reveal that you listen to God's Word in your life? How can you look for God's presence in all the experiences of your life?

Third Sunday of Lent

EXODUS 20:1–17

When the Ten Commandments were given to the Jewish people, it brought them into a covenant with God. Having a covenant with the Lord made the Israelite nation a holy people, chosen to be God's own. In keeping the commandments, Jewish people were able to celebrate their dependence on God and take joy in their special relationship with the Creator and Savior.

- Which of these commandments instruct the people to respect and honor God?
- The rest of the commandments have to do with what type of relationship?
- Why would it have been important for the First Commandment to require reverence to God alone and no other gods?
- Although society today does not publicly worship golden calves or similar gods, what are some gods that people worship?
- Which commandment do you think is the most difficult for society to follow today? Why?
- What does the word *covet* mean?
- Why would coveting be evil?
- Jesus said that the greatest commandment is to love God with all your heart, mind, and soul, and that the second is to love your neighbor as yourself. Are the Ten Commandments similar to or different than this statement? How?

Taking My Scripture Home

Of all the commandments, which one is the most difficult for you to obey? What specific action can you take this Lent to follow that commandment more closely? How can your actions show that you have respect for God, others, and the world?

RESPONSORIAL REFLECTION: JOHN 6:68c

- What are the *words of everlasting life?*
- How do you suppose following God's laws brings about everlasting life?
- What are some life-giving moments you have experienced?

1 CORINTHIANS 1:22–25

St. Paul in this passage speaks of how the heart of the gospel message is foolishness in the eyes of the world. A crucified and risen Christ was not something the Jews, Gentiles, or Greeks looked for in a savior. Yet in this apparent foolishness and weakness is a wisdom and strength far beyond what humanity can grasp.

- Why would the crucifixion of Christ be a stumbling block to anyone?
- What type of person was typically crucified?
- Why do you suppose it was difficult for people to appreciate a God who would die on a cross?
- What are some false expectations people have of God today?
- Why would the suffering and death of Christ be foolish to the Gentiles?
- What is a Gentile?
- During Lent we focus on the Passion and resurrection of Jesus. Why do you think Jesus' death and resurrection are important to Christians?
- Why do you think the secular world fears death?
- In the reading St. Paul points out that the wisdom of God is far above human wisdom. What do you suppose this means?
- What does it mean to say that *God's weakness is stronger than human strength?*

Taking My Scripture Home

St. Paul in this letter to the Corinthians speaks of how God's wisdom is greater than that of the world. What are some ways you have difficulty trusting in the wisdom of God? What can you do to open yourself to trusting God's love more?

JOHN 2:13–25

Lent provides us an opportunity to purify ourselves through prayer, fasting, and sacrifice. The image of Jesus cleansing the temple in this Gospel helps us call to mind those places in our own lives that need cleansing. Consistent with the words of St. Paul in the second reading, the Jews ask Jesus for a sign to explain his actions.

- Why do you suppose Jesus was so upset in the temple?
- What are some ways people today show disregard for God's presence?
- The Jews in the temple demanded Jesus give them a sign to explain his actions. How did Jesus respond?

- Why do you suppose the Jews misunderstood what he was referring to when Jesus said he would raise up the temple in three days?
- Why would Jesus' resurrection convince people he acted in God's name?
- What are some signs today that reveal God's presence?
- What are some expectations or signs that we demand of God?
- This passage speaks of how many people came to believe in Jesus because of the signs he worked. What sort of signs of God's love do you have in your life?
- How do acts of kindness, forgiveness, and compassion strengthen our faith in God?

Taking My Scripture Home

What can you do during Lent to cleanse the temple of your soul? Who in your life is particularly in need of respect, kindness, or compassion? How can you make a difference for this person?

Fourth Sunday of Lent

This Sunday marks the halfway point to our highest and holiest feast of the year, Easter Sunday. Rose-colored vestments may be worn as a reminder to rejoice during this penitential season.

2 CHRONICLES 36:14–16, 19–23

First and Second Chronicles are books of historical writing. Some of the same stories that are found in the books of Samuel and Kings are also found in these books. They were written between 400 and 200 BC by an unknown author or authors.

- What is happening in this story?
- What did God do to try to save the people?
- What did the people do to the prophets?
- What happened next?
- How does this story end?
- In this story God sent messengers to the people. Who are people in our lives who bring God's message to us?
- What are some ways people today mock or turn their backs on God's message?
- What might we expect to happen in our hearts, our families, and our communities when people turn their backs on God's message?
- Where else is this cycle of death and resurrection repeated in Scripture?

Taking My Scripture Home

How can remembering the cycle of death and resurrection help you appreciate sadness? How can unhappy experiences lead to growth opportunities for you? How can this attitude help you the next time something bad happens in your life?

RESPONSORIAL PSALM REFLECTION: PSALM 137:6ab

- Where have you seen examples of people who have forgotten God?
- How can people your age get to a place in their lives where they forget God?
- What happens to us when we forget God?

EPHESIANS 2:4–10

In this passage the author of Ephesians emphasizes how the mercy of God saves us. We are not saved by our own merit. We do not earn God's love or salvation: it is a gift given to us by God.

- What is a transgression?
- How have we been saved?
- What is grace?
- In this reading what are some characteristics of God?
- The author speaks of God's mercy, love, and kindness. Can these characteristics challenge some of your ideas of God? How?
- Does this reading challenge the vision of God as being uncaring, distant, or judgmental? How?
- What are *works* that the author talks about in this reading?
- Why do you think the author points out that we are not saved by works?
- Are works important or not? Explain.
- The author talks about good works that God has prepared for us. What do you think this means?
- Do you think we each have a vocation? Explain.

Taking My Scripture Home

How can focusing on God's mercy, love, and kindness help you when you feel bad about yourself? Are good works a part of your life? How can you discern what to do?

JOHN 3:14–21

Nicodemus was a Pharisee, a leader in the Jewish community, who held a prestigious position. He was a person who was supposed to know all about God's laws and teachings. However, Nicodemus arranged to meet Jesus secretly, at night, to ask questions about God.

- Why do you think Nicodemus came to Jesus at night?
- How do you think Nicodemus's friends and colleagues would have reacted to Nicodemus meeting with Jesus?
- Are there situations today when people are embarrassed to admit they are Christians because of what others might think? Give an example.
- How do you think Nicodemus might have felt when Jesus said that some people prefer darkness?
- Jesus talked about the light coming into the world. What is the light?
- Why would those who love the truth prefer the light?
- Why does it sometimes take courage to have faith?

- In what way was Nicodemus being courageous in this story? In what way was he being a coward?
- What do you think Jesus meant when he talked about how the Son of Man must be lifted up?
- Jesus talks about how God wants to give us eternal life and not condemn us. What does this tell you about how God feels toward us?

Taking My Scripture Home

In what ways can you live in the light? Which of your actions or attitudes would you change if they were exposed for the world to see? How can you be courageous in your faith no matter what others might think of you?

Fifth Sunday of Lent

JEREMIAH 31:31–34

Jeremiah was a prophet, teaching from about 627 BC to 580 BC. Most of these years were before the defeat of Judah and the destruction of the temple. He preached about repentance and judgment; the people did not listen. After the destruction of the temple and the defeat of Judah, his preaching took on a different tone. He preached of hope, encouragement, and a new beginning.

- What was the first covenant that God made with the Jewish people when they were led out of Egypt?
- On what were the commandments written?
- What do you suppose Jeremiah meant by saying the laws of the new covenant will be written on the people's hearts?
- How might someone act if the law of love were written on his or her heart?
- Why do you suppose Jeremiah said that the people no longer needed to teach their friends and relatives how to know the Lord?
- How do people today know if they have broken this interior law?
- How do you suppose the people felt knowing that God would forgive them and not remember their sins?

Taking My Scripture Home

When have you ignored God's law of love that is written on your heart? When are you most likely to ignore the interior law and not open your heart to God and others? How can your actions this week reflect God's interior law?

RESPONSORIAL PSALM REFLECTION: PSALM 51:12a

- How would you describe *a clean heart?*
- What are some characteristics of those who have *a clean heart?*
- How can people allow God to create *a clean heart* in them?

HEBREWS 5:7–9

Hebrews is not really a letter, but a sermon. There is no author mentioned in this book and the authorship is still disputed to this day. Although some traditions assume the author was St. Paul, others believe the book could have been written by Barnabas, Apollos, Priscilla, or Aquila.

- The author writes about Jesus praying with loud cries and tears to God before his death. What does this image of Jesus tell us about what he may have been feeling about the death he was to endure?
- Do these feelings Jesus had make him more able to relate to the suffering, pain, and insecurities we might feel at times? Explain.
- The author writes that Jesus was heard because of his reverence. What is reverence?
- Why would God be more inclined to hear someone who prays with reverence?
- What would be an example of someone praying without reverence?
- What are some ways people might show reverence to those who are suffering in our world?
- This reading also talks about how Jesus learned obedience from what he suffered. Why is obedience a virtue?
- How can our pain and suffering help us grow closer to God?
- How can our pain and suffering help us become more caring and compassionate to others who suffer?

Taking My Scripture Home

In this passage Jesus is reverent and obedient despite his suffering. What can you do to show others that you respect them? How can you show your love for others through obedience? What can you do to help attitudes of obedience and reverence grow in your heart?

JOHN 12:20–33

This event in Jesus' life took place after he had been welcomed into Jerusalem by joyous crowds waving palm branches and before the Last Supper.

- Why must a grain of wheat die in order to produce?
- Why do you think Jesus used this analogy?

- How do these words apply to people today?
- Why do people often have to die to their own wants and desires to lead a Christian life?
- In this passage Jesus says unless a grain of wheat falls to the ground and dies, it remains just a grain of wheat. What are some ways people can be like the wheat that is unwilling to die?
- What are some ways people die to their own wants in order to help others and bring God's love into the world?
- Why do you suppose Jesus said he was troubled?
- How do you suppose Jesus felt knowing the crucifixion was ahead of him?
- How did Jesus glorify God?
- How did Jesus' crucifixion draw people together?

Taking My Scripture Home

What are some of your own wants and desires that, if given up, could have a positive effect on others? How can you bring others to God's love?

Passion/Palm Sunday

ISAIAH 50:4—7

This passage is read every year on Passion/Palm Sunday. In the book of Isaiah there are four sections called the "Servant Songs." These four passages describe the perfect servant of God. Although these descriptions are similar to those of Jesus' life, many believe the "servant" to be the Church.

- How does this reading describe the servant's relationship to God?
- How often does this servant listen to the Word of God?
- How often do we listen to the Word of God?
- The servant brings God's Word to others. How can we bring God's Word to other people?
- In the reading the servant allows his beard to be plucked. In Isaiah's time this was the worse insult a person could receive. What are some ways society insults people today?
- In our own lives how do we insult others?
- The reading ends with the statement that the servant will not be put to shame. Why should this statement give us hope?

Taking My Scripture Home

During this upcoming week, when can you take the time to listen to God? How can you bring God's message of love to others?

RESPONSORIAL PSALM REFLECTION: PSALM 22:2a

- Where else in the Bible can we read these words?
- Although this statement seems as if God has turned his back on the Psalmist,

the entire Psalm is about hoping in God. Why would Jesus have begun to recite this Psalm when dying on the cross?
- What do you suppose would be God's answer to this Psalm?

PHILIPPIANS 2:6–11

This second reading is also read each Passion/Palm Sunday. The book of Philippians is a letter written by St. Paul to the people of Philippi. Scholars believe it was written between AD 57 and 63 while St. Paul was in prison for preaching the gospel. This passage is thought to have been a hymn that was cited by St. Paul.

- In what ways could Jesus have shown his equality with God?
- How do people try to be *god-like* today?
- Why is humility important?
- This reading speaks of Jesus being obedient to the point of death. Why is obedience a virtue?
- How can our obedience help spread God's love to others?
- What does the word *exalt* mean?
- What type of things does society exalt?
- How is this different than what Jesus did?
- How did God exalt Jesus?

Taking My Scripture Home

What are some ways in your own life that you forget to exalt the humble? In what ways do your actions and attitudes reflect *selfishness?* How can you become more humble?

GOSPEL

Because of the length of this reading, it can be read and reflected on in smaller passages. The Passion narrative is rich with vivid images of Jesus' suffering and invites us to quiet meditation. Therefore, the "Taking My Scripture Home" section is omitted this Sunday.

Mark 14:1–11

- What was Jesus' attitude toward the woman in this passage?
- What did others think of the woman's actions?
- What do you suppose was the woman's motive?
- Why is it important to look for the good in those around us?
- Why were the chief priests pleased with Judas?
- What was Judas's motive?

Mark 14:12–21

- Who betrayed Jesus?
- Why do you think Judas came back to eat the Passover with Jesus and the disciples?
- How do you think Jesus felt knowing Judas would betray him?

Mark 14:22–31

- How do you think Jesus felt knowing it was the last time he would eat with his friends?

Mark 14:32–42

- What do you suppose Jesus was feeling as he prayed in the garden?
- Why did Jesus pray, . . . *but not what I will, but what you will?*
- How can Jesus' example help you deal with difficult things in your life?

Mark 14:43–52

- Why do you think Judas betrayed Jesus?
- How do you think Jesus felt when Judas kissed him?
- What are some ways people betray others with their actions and words?
- Why did Jesus not want violence used to protect him?
- What are some Christian ways to respond to those who hurt you?

Mark 14:53–65

- How do you think Jesus felt when the leaders were trying to make up stories to use against him?
- Why do you suppose the Jewish religious leaders asked Jesus if he was the Messiah?
- Why were they trying to trap Jesus?
- How do you think it feels to be accused of something you did not do?

Mark 14:66–72

- What happened to make Peter go from courageously supporting Jesus to denying him three times?
- When is it easy to follow Jesus and when is it difficult?
- How do you suppose Peter felt after he denied Jesus and remembered that Jesus had predicted the denial?

Mark 15:1–21

- How do you suppose Jesus felt when the crowd shouted for him to be crucified even though everyone knew he was innocent?

- How do you respond when people treat you unjustly?
- Why would Pilate give in to the demands of the crowd and let them crucify Jesus?
- What are some examples of how peer pressure affects you and your friends?

Mark 15:22–41

- Why did the centurion believe in Jesus' innocence?
- How did those who mocked Jesus' crucifixion feel after Jesus died?
- How do you suppose the friends of Jesus felt watching him from a distance?

Mark 15:42–47

- Why would it be uncharacteristic for a distinguished member of the council to worry about burying Jesus?
- How do you suppose Joseph of Arimathea felt about what happened to Jesus?
- How can his example help you stand up for people who are being treated unjustly?

Conclusion

The Passion gives us a clear picture of the unjust and cruel things that happened to Jesus before his death. However, we know this is not the end of the story. How can knowing that Jesus suffered and died—but that was not the end—help you when you are going through difficulties?

Easter Sunday

These readings are taken from the Mass During the Day.

ACTS 10:34a, 37–43

In this passage St. Peter is speaking to a group of Gentiles. At the time the gospel message was thought to be only for the Jewish people, not Gentiles. St. Peter, in a vision, was told by God to convey the gospel message to Gentiles as well as Jews. After St. Peter's speech the Gentiles received the Holy Spirit.

- This speech by St. Peter is a brief summary of Jesus' life. What are some of the things St. Peter left out of the speech?
- How do you think the listeners knew what had happened to Jesus?
- In his speech St. Peter mentions that God chose him and the other disciples to witness to all that Jesus did and to preach his message to all people. How does the Church continue this mission today?
- What do you suppose was the most radical message Jesus taught?
- What are some ways people your age can show others what Jesus taught?
- St. Peter talks about how God raised Jesus from the dead. Why do you suppose Jesus' resurrection was so important to the Christian faith?
- What does Jesus' resurrection say about the truth of all that he preached?
- How do you feel knowing that everyone who believes in Jesus will receive forgiveness for his or her sins?
- Why do you suppose this news of forgiveness and Jesus' resurrection is difficult for some people to believe?

Taking My Scripture Home

Jesus' resurrection assures us of a wonderful life that awaits us beyond this life. How does your life reflect that you believe in this joyful message? How can you help others believe in this good news?

RESPONSORIAL PSALM REFLECTION: PSALM 118:24

- What does it mean to say that *this is the day the Lord has made?*
- How does Jesus' resurrection fill us with joy?
- How can we share this resurrection joy with others?

1 CORINTHIANS 5:6b–8

In this passage St. Paul uses the example of yeast because it was very familiar to the Corinthians. Yeast represents corruption or wrongdoing in this reading. Unleavened bread is bread with no yeast.

- What does it mean when someone says, "One bad apple can spoil the barrel"?
- How is that saying similar to the analogy St. Paul is using in this reading?
- How do you think a small amount of yeast can affect all the dough in bread?
- What does a small amount of corruption do to a person?
- What are some attitudes or actions that are examples of corruption?
- What happens to a community when people treat each other with malice or disrespect?
- St. Paul talks about celebrating the feast with the unleavened bread of sincerity and truth. Why is it important to try to purify ourselves?
- What season of the liturgical cycle is set aside for us to purify ourselves before we celebrate the feast of Jesus' resurrection?
- What are some attitudes and actions that reveal a pure heart?
- What happens to a community when people treat each other with compassion and respect?

Taking My Scripture Home

St. Paul talks about the influence of a little yeast among the dough. How can you be a good influence on those you meet? What can you do to keep your thoughts and intentions pure? What can you do to resist those who might act with disrespect or malice toward others?

JOHN 20:1–9

Easter is the highest feast of the year and the celebration begins at the Easter Vigil Mass on Saturday evening. The Easter Vigil Gospel, Mark 16:1–7, may be substituted for this Gospel during the Mass of Easter Day.

- Why do you think Mary Magdalene went to the tomb that morning?
- What do you suppose she thought when she discovered the tomb was open?
- After St. Peter and the other disciple heard the news, what happened next that shows they acted with urgency?

- How did the other disciple react when he arrived at the tomb?
- What did St. Peter do?
- What does this tell us about St. Peter's personality?
- What are some other impulsive, bold decisions St. Peter made in other gospel stories?
- Why do you think such a vivid description is given about the burial cloths?
- This story ends with the other disciple going into the tomb, seeing, and believing, yet not understanding. Is it possible to believe without understanding? Explain.
- How did Jesus' resurrection change things for the followers of Jesus?
- This story is filled with common emotions that we all feel. What are some of these emotions?

Taking My Scripture Home

What signs of Jesus' resurrection do you see in your life? How can you use these signs to remind yourself of God's love? How can you share God's love with others through your actions and attitudes?

Second Sunday of Easter

Traditionally this Sunday has been called Low Sunday because it follows Easter, the highest feast of the year. More recently, at the suggestion of Pope John Paul II, it is also known as Divine Mercy Sunday.

ACTS 4:32–35

St. Luke in this passage describes the amazing charity of the early Christians who took Jesus' message of sharing to heart. This passage provides a good insight into how the early Christians viewed themselves as one united body of believers.

- What do you suppose it means to have a community of people believing they are of one mind and heart?
- Do you know of any examples of communities in today's world that see themselves this way?
- What keeps people today from seeing themselves as united with others?
- How would the world be different if everyone acted with the same cooperative spirit as the early Church?
- Imagine what it is like to live in a community where everything is shared and everyone's needs are met. What role does faith and trust play in keeping a community such as this together?
- What can people do to increase their dependence on God?
- How can people develop their ability to recognize their own goodness and the goodness of others?

Taking My Scripture Home

What can you do this week to reach out with trust and charity to others? Who is a person in your life with whom you have a strained relationship? What good, wonder, and talents does that person possess?

RESPONSORIAL PSALM REFLECTION: PSALM 118:1

- How do you give thanks to the Lord?
- What does it mean to say that the Lord is good?
- What must it be like to experience everlasting love?

1 JOHN 5:1–6

This letter was written around AD 100 by either the writer of the Gospel of John or one of his close followers. This letter tries to develop more fully the spiritual life of the community and to correct some misconceptions about Jesus.

- What does it mean to believe that Jesus is the Christ?
- What are the commandments that God wants us to keep?
- What are some examples of how people today keep these commandments?
- What are some struggles that people your age face in trying to keep God's commandments?
- Why do you suppose the author wrote that God's commandments are not burdensome?
- What does it mean to be *begotten by God?*
- How do those who are *begotten by God* conquer the world?
- What does it mean to say *Jesus came through water and blood?*

Taking My Scripture Home

Who in your life is a good example of someone who keeps God's commandments? How can that person be a role model for you?

JOHN 20:19–31

This is a busy passage that holds many significant events. Jesus' appearance to the disciples, his giving of the Holy Spirit, his commissioning them to go forth, and Thomas's doubts are all captured in a few short paragraphs. Interestingly, Thomas's name means twin, yet nowhere in Scripture is there mention of a twin brother. Folklore has suggested that perhaps anyone who entertains doubt or requires proof of Jesus' resurrection may be Thomas's unmentioned twin.

- How would you describe the feelings the disciples had while they were hiding in the room before Jesus appeared?
- How did these feelings change when Jesus appeared?
- Why do you suppose their feelings changed?
- What did Jesus intend the disciples to do when he sent them forth?
- Why did Jesus breathe on them and give them the Holy Spirit?
- Why didn't Thomas believe that the other disciples had seen Jesus?

- Why is it difficult for people to believe that Jesus rose from the dead and forgives sin?
- What did Jesus mean when he said that blessed are those who believe without seeing?
- What do you think is the most compelling reason for believing in Jesus?

Taking My Scripture Home

What are some doubts about your faith that cause you to struggle? What is it about the story of Jesus' life that gives you most hope?

Third Sunday of Easter

ACTS 3:13–15, 17–19

This speech by St. Peter was addressed to the Jewish people in Solomon's Portico in the temple. Peter and John were entering the temple to attend three o'clock prayer when a crippled man asked them for alms. Peter healed the man, who in turn was filled with joy and clung to Peter as he made this speech before the Jews.

- Why would St. Peter emphasize to this group that the God of Abraham, Isaac, and Jacob had glorified Jesus?
- How would you describe the tone of this speech? Explain.
- What are some actions and attitudes that attempt to put to death God's message of love?
- The Jews who were gathered around St. Peter were amazed at the miraculous healing of the crippled man that had just taken place. How do you think they felt listening to his words?
- What was the reason St. Peter made this speech? What did he want the Jewish people to do?
- What does it mean to repent and be converted?
- Is conversion a one-time occurrence, or is it something that is ongoing? Explain.

Taking My Scripture Home

What attitudes or perspectives do you feel need to be converted in your life? What can you do to open your heart more fully to God?

RESPONSORIAL PSALM REFLECTION: PSALM 4:7a

- Why is there goodness in the face of God?
- Why does the Psalmist ask God to shine on all of us instead of just himself?
- How has the Lord's face shone in your life?

1 JOHN 2:1–5a

The theme of keeping God's commandments is taken up again this week in John's first letter. While he addressed the group as though they were children, he was actually addressing adults. It was customary to use that term to convey endearment and love. In this passage John is trying to emphasize the importance of obedience to God.

- John claims to be writing to keep the people from sinning. What does it mean to sin?
- What is an advocate?
- How does Jesus serve as an advocate to God for our sins?
- What are the commandments Jesus asks us to keep?
- How does keeping God's commandments assure us that we know God?
- What do you call a person who claims to be Christian yet never acts in ways that are consistent with the gospel?
- What actions and attitudes might you expect to find in someone who truly keeps God's commandments?
- Why do you suppose John said the love of God is perfected in those who keep God's Word?

Taking My Scripture Home

When do you find it most difficult to keep God's commandment of love and respect? How can you make a special effort to let God's love live in you the next time you find yourself in a difficult situation?

LUKE 24:35–48

This appearance to all of the disciples was yet more proof that Jesus had risen from the dead and helped validate all that he had taught them while they were together. Each of the gospel writers includes episodes of Jesus appearing to the disciples after his resurrection.

- What effect did this appearance of Jesus have upon the disciples?
- Why was it important for Jesus to let the disciples touch him and eat with him?
- What sort of questions would you have asked Jesus if you had been one of the disciples gathered there on that day?

- Why do you suppose Jesus opened their minds to the Scriptures and reminded them of how he was the fulfillment of the prophets, the law of Moses, and the Psalms?
- If you were one of the disciples, what sort of impact would this experience have had on your faith in Jesus?
- The disciples had the advantage of experiencing Jesus' resurrection first-hand. What are some ways people today experience God's love, generosity, and forgiveness firsthand?
- Why is the forgiveness of sins such good news?

Taking My Scripture Home

What is it about the Gospels that causes you to believe in Jesus? Who are the people in your life that have encouraged and nurtured your faith? How can you share your joy of forgiveness with other people?

Fourth Sunday of Easter

ACTS 4:8–12

St. Peter had just healed a crippled man he had encountered upon entering the temple. Soon a crowd gathered and he used the occasion to preach about Jesus (see the first reading from last Sunday.) The priests, the captain of the temple guard, and the Sadducees came and arrested Peter and John. The next day they asked Peter on whose authority he had healed the crippled man. This passage is Peter's response before the Sanhedrin.

- How do you suppose the Jewish leaders responded to the testimony St. Peter made about Jesus in this passage?
- What does it mean to say that Jesus was the stone they rejected?
- What are some ways people today reject Jesus or his teaching?
- What does it mean to say Jesus became the cornerstone?
- What are some ways people today can make Jesus the cornerstone of their lives?
- St. Peter healed a crippled man in the name of Jesus. How can those who truly live Christ's teachings bring healing to people today?
- What did St. Peter mean by saying that there is no other name by which we are to be saved?

Taking My Scripture Home

What can you do to make Jesus' teaching of forgiveness and compassion the cornerstone of your life? How can you bring healing to others?

RESPONSORIAL PSALM REFLECTION: PSALM 118:22

- How does this response reflect the difference between humanity's values and God's values?
- What is the building where Jesus has been placed as the cornerstone?
- How can your attitudes and actions help build God's kingdom?

1 JOHN 3:1—2

Throughout this letter John contrasts the differences between the world and the ways of Christians. This passage is a good example of how that theme is woven into so much of his teaching.

- How has God bestowed love on people?
- Why do you suppose Christians can be called children of God?
- What does it mean to be God's children?
- How can you tell by someone's actions and attitudes if he or she is a child of God?
- Why did John say that the world did not know God?
- What was John referring to when he said what we are to be has not been revealed?
- What can people do to follow Jesus more closely?

Taking My Scripture Home

What are some ways you have experienced God's love in your life? How is God's love revealed to you through the people who love you?

JOHN 10:11—18

The Fourth Sunday of Easter is known as Good Shepherd Sunday. Each year on this Sunday a passage is read from the Gospel that explores the image of Jesus as the shepherd of the flock. The other sheep mentioned in this passage probably refer to the Gentiles.

- What are some qualities of a good shepherd?
- Why do you suppose Jesus used this image to speak of himself?
- How does this image of God as a good shepherd differ from other images people might have of God?
- What does this passage imply about Jesus' plan for the unity of all people?
- How do people hear Jesus' voice today?
- What sacrifice did Jesus make for his flock?
- What are some sacrifices people your age might have to make in order to follow Jesus more closely?

Taking My Scripture Home

Who are the people in your life that lead you? Do these people lead you to a closer relationship with God?

Fifth Sunday of Easter

ACTS 9:26–31

The man named Saul in this passage later changed his name to Paul. Today he is revered as "St. Paul." St. Paul is the writer of most of the letters of the New Testament. Saul had been a persecutor of the Christians, seeking them out and murdering them. He had just undergone a conversion and baptism when he arrived in Jerusalem. Naturally his previous reputation preceded him and instilled fear in the disciples. The Hellenists were Greek-speaking Jews living in Jerusalem.

- Saul had just undergone an amazing conversion and yet the disciples did not believe him. Why were the disciples so afraid of Saul?
- What effect do mistrust and fear have on a community?
- Why do you suppose Barnabas took responsibility for Saul and brought him to the Apostles?
- How do you suppose Saul felt when Barnabas decided to trust him and bring him to the Apostles?
- Why is it important to be able to see the good in others?
- This passage speaks of how the Church was growing and walking in the fear of the Lord. What does it mean to walk in the fear of the Lord?
- How do people your age show respect to God?

Taking My Scripture Home

Who is someone in your life that has trusted you and seen the goodness in you? How can you develop your ability to see good in others?

RESPONSORIAL PSALM REFLECTION: PSALM 22:26a

- How do you praise the Lord?
- Why do you praise the Lord?
- Why is it good to praise the Lord in a community?

1 JOHN 3:18–24

In this passage St. John speaks of the importance of obedience to God. He summarizes the heart of the Gospels by emphasizing the greatest of the commandments.

- How do people love in deed and truth?
- Why is it more important to love in deed than in word or speech?
- What does it mean to say that *our hearts do not condemn us?*
- According to this passage what are the two simple laws on which we can build our conscience?
- What does it mean to believe in Jesus Christ?
- Why is belief in Jesus Christ important?
- If we believe in Jesus and love others, then God lives in us according to this passage. What does it mean to truly love others?
- How does God's Spirit help a person become more loving?

Taking My Scripture Home

What are some things you have done in your life that might be considered loving actions? How did your actions bring about good to others? What are some other ways you can share God's Spirit of love?

JOHN 15:1–8

The rich symbolism of this passage is reminiscent of the many parables Jesus used throughout his ministry. The vivid imagery of these stories and the connections with examples from the everyday life of the common people of Jesus' time made parables an especially effective means of teaching. The people could relate to the stories and could easily remember the imagery.

- What is Jesus referring to when he speaks of bearing fruit?
- What are some ways people today bear fruit for God?
- What do you suppose Jesus is referring to when he says those branches that bear fruit will be pruned in order to bear more fruit?
- What are some disciplines people endure today in order to become better?
- How would you explain what Jesus meant by saying we cannot bear fruit unless we remain in him?
- How do people remain in Jesus?

- What did Jesus mean when he said if we remain in him, whatever we ask will be done for us?
- According to this passage who is responsible for the good that people do? Explain.

Taking My Scripture Home

What can you do to let God's love shine more brightly through you? What are some struggles you have faced that might be considered spiritual pruning?

Sixth Sunday of Easter

ACTS 10:25–26, 34–35, 44–48

Cornelius was a devout and God-fearing Gentile. While he was praying an angel instructed him to send for St. Peter. Before Peter met with Cornelius, he received a vision that encouraged him to accept the Gentiles into the Christian community. This passage begins with Peter's entrance into Cornelius's home, where many people had gathered to hear his words. The reading picks up with a portion of Peter's speech and concludes with a description of Cornelius's baptism.

- Why do you suppose Cornelius fell to St. Peter's feet and paid him homage?
- How do people today express their respect for one another?
- How did St. Peter respond to Cornelius's gesture?
- What did St. Peter's actions and words reveal about his humility?
- What does it mean to fear God and act uprightly?
- The circumcised Jewish believers were astonished to see the Holy Spirit had been poured out on a Gentile. Why do you suppose these believers were astonished?
- What notions do people have today that put limits on God's love and power?

Taking My Scripture Home

What is it about God's love, power, or creativity that astonishes you? How do you show respect and awe for God's goodness?

RESPONSORIAL PSALM REFLECTION: PSALM 98:2b

- What is the Lord's saving power?
- How has the Lord revealed this *saving power?*
- What effect does the Lord's saving power have in your life?

1 JOHN 4:7–10

This passage from John's first letter is taken from his teaching about how to test if spirits are from God or from the world. This passage affirms that love is a spirit that comes from God.

- How would you describe the spirit of love?
- What does it mean to say that *love is of God?*
- What are some ways God's spirit of love works through people today?
- Why might people today be without love?
- Is it possible to express love if a person has never experienced love first?
- How do people experience God's love today?
- How is forgiveness an expression of love?

Taking My Scripture Home

Who in your life has been a strong source of God's love? How can you reflect that love to others through your actions and attitudes?

JOHN 15:9–17

This passage is a continuation of last Sunday's Gospel and builds on this Sunday's theme of the importance of love. Jesus speaks of the relationship with God as one of friendship instead of slavery. Jesus' words help us understand that each of us is called to a more intimate and personal relationship with God.

- How are people supposed to remain in God's love?
- What are the commandments that we are required to keep?
- Why do you suppose Jesus puts so much emphasis on loving others?
- Why is laying down one's life for another the greatest sign of love?
- How do people today lay down their lives for others?
- Jesus told the disciples everything he had heard from God. Why would this willingness to share everything make them friends?
- What did Jesus want the disciples to do with the information he shared with them?
- How can people today bear fruit for God and share this message of love?

Taking My Scripture Home

How can you act in the best interest of others without concern for your own interests? How is that like laying down your life for others?

The Ascension of the Lord

ACTS 1:1–11

The book of Acts, or Acts of the Apostles, was written by the author of the Gospel of Luke to continue the story after Jesus' death and resurrection. In this passage Luke sets the context for the book of Acts by summarizing the final events in the Gospel of Luke: the appearances of Jesus to the disciples and the ascension of Jesus.

- This book begins by referring to the first book, the book of Luke. What are some things Jesus taught in this Gospel?
- How do you suppose the disciples felt when Jesus appeared to them?
- Jesus tells the disciples that they will receive power with the Holy Spirit. What types of things did the disciples do with this power?
- How can we use the power of the Holy Spirit today?
- Do you think this power is available to everyone? Explain.
- How does one receive this power?
- How do you think the disciples felt when Jesus ascended to heaven?
- Why do you suppose the two men appeared and spoke to them?

Taking My Scripture Home

Do you really believe in the power of the Holy Spirit? How can you use this power to spread God's love to all people?

RESPONSORIAL PSALM REFLECTION: PSALM 47:6

- What images of God does this Psalm bring to mind?
- Why would there be shouts of joy and music in God's presence?
- How can we display this enthusiasm for God's reign in our everyday lives?

EPHESIANS 4:1–13

This passage was chosen for the feast because it speaks of Christ who descended and ascended. The gifts of the Spirit are given to help the faithful build up God's kingdom.

- What do you suppose the author means when he writes about the call the readers received?
- Do you think God still calls people today? Explain.
- The author describes characteristics worthy of the call of God. How are living these characteristics a call for all people?
- How would the world be different if each person tried to live up to these characteristics?
- The author explains how Jesus ascended and descended. How can this give us faith in the power of God?
- How can faith in God help us follow God no matter what happens in our lives?

Taking My Scripture Home

What do you believe God is calling you to do? How can you live in a way that takes that call seriously?

MARK 16:15–20

In this passage the disciples are commissioned and Jesus ascends to heaven and sits at God's right hand. The Gospel of Mark ends with these verses.

- What did Jesus tell the disciples to do?
- What are some ways the disciples spread God's message of love to others?
- What are some ways people today can spread the message of God's love in their everyday lives?
- Jesus talks of miracles that are associated with God's people. What are some examples of miracles that have happened to Christians?
- How do these miracles encourage us to be faithful and obey God?
- What are some miracles that happen around us each day?
- How do you think the disciples felt when Jesus ascended to heaven?
- What does it mean to sit at someone's right hand?

Taking My Scripture Home

How do you spread the message of God's love each day? How does it feel to know that Jesus, who sits at God's right hand, loves you enough to die for you?

Pentecost

These readings are taken from the Mass During the Day.

ACTS 2:1–11

Pentecost took place in the city of Jerusalem, where the disciples had gathered to pray. After Judas's betrayal and suicide, there were only eleven remaining disciples. To keep the number of disciples at twelve, they appointed a new disciple, Matthias. The coming of the Holy Spirit was recorded after this event.

- Luke writes of wind and fire. What senses would someone use when experiencing wind and fire?
- Why do you think Luke wrote of the presence of these elements at Pentecost?
- The Holy Spirit allowed the disciples to speak in different tongues. How do you think the disciples felt when speaking in languages they did not know?
- What powerful images of the Holy Spirit does this event bring to mind?
- Why do you suppose the Holy Spirit chose the twelve disciples? What role, if any, do you think prayer had in the Holy Spirit's coming?
- How do you think those who were in the crowd felt when they witnessed such amazing powers?
- With the power of the Holy Spirit the disciples were able to perform deeds that they could not perform without this power. How does the Holy Spirit empower us today?

Taking My Scripture Home

Do you pray each day for the power of the Holy Spirit? How can this power help you in your choices, decisions, and daily activities?

RESPONSORIAL PSALM REFLECTION: PSALM 104:30

- Why is it important to ask God to send the Holy Spirit?
- If the Holy Spirit was present in everyone each day, how would the world be different?
- How does God's Spirit renew the Earth?

GALATIANS 5:16–25

St. Paul wrote the letter to the Galatians at a time when many of the churches he had founded were being influenced by other traditions and cultures. Many churches had begun to add laws and practices to their Christianity. There has always been a temptation to rely on laws and externals in religious life, often to the neglect of things of the Spirit. St. Paul, in this passage, challenges the Galatians to avoid becoming overly dependent on the law.

- Why do you think St. Paul was so thorough in explaining the differences between the desires of the flesh and the Spirit?
- What are some situations where the desires of the flesh are apparent in today's society?
- What are some examples of events where the Spirit is at work in society today?
- What does it mean to not be *under the law?*
- Why would someone who was guided and motivated by the Spirit not need to worry about what the law considers to be right or wrong?
- St. Paul lists the fruits of the Spirit in this passage. Who do you know in your own life that possesses these characteristics?
- Six of the seven fruits of the Holy Spirit are behaviors or ways to conduct one's self. Which of the fruits listed can be chosen or developed?
- Why is it important to ask for the Spirit's guidance each day?

Taking My Scripture Home

Which of your attitudes or actions do you feel need to be guided by the Spirit? How can you open your heart to the Spirit and choose to respond to situations and events in a more peaceful way?

JOHN 15:26–27; 16:12–15

Jesus speaks this passage in John's Gospel during the Last Supper. Jesus had washed the disciples' feet, and Judas had left to betray him.

- What is an advocate?
- What is Jesus talking about when he speaks of the Advocate?

- Why do you suppose it was important that Jesus told the disciples the Advocate would be sent to them?
- What happened to Jesus after the Last Supper?
- How do you think the disciples felt when they remembered Jesus' words after he died?
- What happened on Pentecost?
- How does the Holy Spirit guide us to truth?

Taking My Scripture Home

How can the image of the Holy Spirit as an advocate help you open your heart to the Spirit? How can the Holy Spirit strengthen you to spread God's message?

Second Sunday of Ordinary Time

1 SAMUEL 3:3b–10, 19

This passage tells of an event in the early life of the prophet Samuel. Samuel's mother, Hannah, had promised God that she would dedicate her first son to the Lord's service. After giving birth to Samuel, Hannah fulfilled her promise to God by taking him to the temple to live and serve with the high priest, Eli. This passage tells of Samuel's call from God.

- In the reading who did Samuel think was calling him?
- After being woken up three times, what did Eli tell Samuel to say?
- How important is it to listen to God?
- How do you think God speaks to us today?
- Why is it important to take time each day to pray and to listen to God?
- What does this passage say about the effectiveness of Samuel's words?
- Do you think that taking time to listen to God can improve our speech or remarks? Explain.

Taking My Scripture Home

How often do you take time to listen to God? How does your speech reveal God's presence in your life?

RESPONSORIAL PSALM REFLECTION: PSALM 40:8a, 9a

- What do you suppose is the Lord's will in your life?
- How can you follow that will each day?
- What are some things that make you less likely to follow God?

1 CORINTHIANS 6:13c–15a, 17–20

St. Paul established a Christian community in Corinth in AD 51. While in Ephesus, St. Paul heard disturbing news about the church in Corinth, which prompted this instructional letter written in AD 56. In this passage St. Paul addresses concerns about sexual immorality in the community.

- St. Paul speaks of how our bodies are for the Lord and how we are to glorify God with our bodies. How would we use our bodies for the Lord?
- How can we glorify God with our bodies?
- What are ways people today show lack of respect for their bodies?
- Why does St. Paul believe that a body is a temple?
- Do you believe all people have the Holy Spirit inside them?
- Why should we consider all people *temples?*
- How should this dictate our treatment of all people?

Taking My Scripture Home

Who in your life do you fail to recognize as a *temple?* How can remembering that each person houses the Holy Spirit help you respect all people?

JOHN 1:35–42

This passage from the early part of John's Gospel describes the beginning of Jesus' ministry and his call to the disciples. Andrew's willingness to follow Jesus and his desire to share his discovery with his brother exemplify the qualities of discipleship.

- The author says that two of John's disciples left him to follow Jesus when John pointed out that Jesus was the Lamb of God. Why would the two disciples have followed Jesus?
- What did Jesus ask the two disciples?
- How do you suppose the two disciples answered?
- What do you think was missing from their lives?
- What are some things commonly missing from people's lives today?
- What do you think people today are looking for?
- The Gospel says that Andrew told his brother, Simon Peter, about Jesus. What are some ways you can tell others of God's love?
- The disciples changed their lives in order to follow Jesus. How does Jesus call us to change?

Taking My Scripture Home

How would you answer the question, "What are you looking for?" How is God calling you to change?

Third Sunday of Ordinary Time

JONAH 3:1–5, 10

The book of Jonah is a parable or historical Midrash and is not to be taken as a record of actual events. Although the author is unknown, this humorous tale was written for the Israelites to demonstrate God's love for all people. Nineveh was a very important city in Assyria, notorious for its decadent lifestyle. Although God told Jonah to preach to the Ninevites, Jonah was reluctant. Jonah believed the people of Nineveh were unworthy of God's love and forgiveness. In this passage, Jonah preaches and the people of Nineveh repent.

- Jonah did not want to preach to the people of Nineveh because he thought they were undeserving of God's love and forgiveness. Where have you seen prejudices in today's society?
- What happened when Jonah put his prejudices aside?
- How can we convey God's unconditional love to all people?
- How can treating all people as God's family help us to be better Christians?
- What does God's forgiveness toward the Ninevites tell us about God?

Taking My Scripture Home

What can you do each day to keep your mind and actions free of discrimination? What are some examples in your own life when you communicate God's unconditional love to others?

RESPONSORIAL PSALM REFLECTION: PSALM 25:4a

- What are God's ways?
- How can you incorporate God's ways into your daily life?
- What are some ways God teaches us?

1 CORINTHIANS 7:29–31

In this passage St. Paul believes the second coming of Christ will happen at any moment. He advises the Corinthian church to stay focused on God's kingdom and to not be distracted by concerns of this world.

- Why do you suppose the tone of St. Paul's letter is so urgent?
- What changes do you suppose people would make in their lives if they believed Christ would return tomorrow?
- What worries of today would be pointless if Christ returned tomorrow?
- Do you believe Christ is present in the world today? Explain.
- Where can we find Christ's presence in our daily lives?

Taking My Scripture Home

Which of your worries are actually pointless? What can you do each day to remember to search for Christ's presence in the world around you?

MARK 1:14–20

In this passage Jesus calls his first disciples and begins his public ministry. He asks the disciples to leave behind everything and share a role in his ministry. Jesus does not begin his public ministry until John the Baptist's public ministry has ended.

- What does it mean to repent?
- Jesus tells the people of Galilee to believe in the gospel. What do you suppose this means?
- In this passage Simon, Andrew, James, and John leave behind their fishing businesses to follow Jesus. Why do you suppose they were willing to leave their livelihoods?
- What might have attracted them to Jesus?
- How do you think their families felt when they announced they were leaving?
- What are some things Christians leave behind to follow God?
- What does it mean to follow God?
- What is a fisher of men?
- What sort of things do people cling to today that make it difficult for them to follow Christ's teachings?

Taking My Scripture Home

What do you need to leave behind to become a better Christian? How can you rely more on God and less on yourself? What are some ways you can ask the Holy Spirit to strengthen your ability to trust God?

Fourth Sunday of Ordinary Time

DEUTERONOMY 18:15–20

The book of Deuteronomy was written before the Israelites entered the Promised Land to remind them of the importance of their covenant with God. The Apostles and the Jewish people understood that this prophet would be raised up from their people and that he would be the Messiah.

- In this passage Moses speaks of a prophet who is like him. What was special about Moses?
- In today's society who would be a prophet like Moses?
- In this passage the people asked for a prophet to speak God's words instead of hearing them directly from God. How do we hear God's voice today?
- This passage also speaks of false prophets—those who say they are speaking in God's name, but are not. Where or in whom do we find false prophets in today's society?
- What are some ways to discern if a message is from God?

Taking My Scripture Home

To whom or what do you listen? Are the messages you receive consistent with Christian values? How can you become better at discerning the voices of society?

RESPONSORIAL PSALM REFLECTION: PSALM 95:8

- Where do you hear God's voice?
- What does it mean to have a hardened heart?
- How can you open your heart to God?

1 CORINTHIANS 7:32–35

This passage is a continuation of the second reading of the Third Sunday of Ordinary Time. St. Paul believes the second coming of Christ will happen at any moment. Therefore, instead of concerning ourselves with the things of this world, the focus should be on the coming of God's kingdom.

- St. Paul speaks of the distraction of being married. What are some things in today's society that distract people from God?
- What are some typical distractions people your age face each day?
- What are some daily habits that could keep people your age focused on God?
- What are some characteristics of people who focus on the things of this world or do not keep their concentration on Christian values?
- St. Paul speaks of those who are anxious about worldly concerns or about the concerns of God. How can you tell if someone is anxious about worldly concerns?

Taking My Scripture Home

What are some ways you can maintain your focus on God? How can you come to recognize the distractions of society that take your focus off God?

MARK 1:21–28

In this passage Jesus is shown as the teacher and healer of unclean spirits. His teaching with authority and his power over unclean spirits set Jesus apart from the scribes. The unclean spirit attempted to name Jesus as the Holy One of God because it believed that saying the name would give power over the individual. Even this attempt to thwart Jesus' power was unsuccessful.

- In this passage the people are amazed by Jesus' teaching because he teaches with authority. What do you suppose this means?
- What are some examples in your own life when someone has spoken with authority?
- What are some characteristics of someone who speaks with authority?
- In Jesus' time scribes were educated men who knew God's Word because they copied the words of the Sacred Scriptures. Why do you think Jesus' teaching was different from that of the scribes?
- What had Jesus actually seen that the scribes had not?
- In this passage Jesus heals a man who had an unclean spirit. What are some unclean spirits we see in today's society?
- Do you think Jesus still heals unclean spirits today? Explain.

Taking My Scripture Home

Are you amazed at the teachings of Jesus? How can you become more attentive to Jesus' message? How can you share Jesus' message at school and at home?

Fifth Sunday of Ordinary Time

JOB 7:1–4, 6–7

The book of Job is a story of a godly man, Job, who goes through tremendous loss, pain, and suffering. In this passage Job is distressed over the loss of his family, fortune, livelihood, and health. These trials and tribulations test Job's faith, yet through it all he remains faithful to God and eventually is given a larger family, more fortune, and good health. The reading this week invites us to reflect on the dark moments of Job's struggle.

- How does Job describe his life?
- How would you feel if you were Job?
- In this passage Job is distraught. Eventually, he does see happiness again. In today's society why is it important to remember that no matter how distressing a situation might be, there is hope for the future?
- What are some ways we can help others when they are distressed?
- How can a strong faith help us see the light at the end of the tunnel?

Taking My Scripture Home

How can remembering the story of Job help when you are depressed or sad? What is positive and hopeful in your life? How can focusing on what is positive and hopeful in your life help you when you are down?

RESPONSORIAL PSALM REFLECTION: PSALM 147:3a

- Who are the brokenhearted in today's society?
- How can a broken heart be healed?
- How does knowing God bring peace?

1 CORINTHIANS 9:16–19, 22–23

In this passage St. Paul explains that his motive for preaching the gospel is not profit or reward, but because the message has been entrusted to him by God. He speaks of his freedom to become a slave or servant to all people.

- In this reading St. Paul refers to preaching the gospel as an obligation. What does this mean?
- What are other obligations associated with being a Christian?
- St. Paul goes on to explain how he is *free in regard to all.* He does not owe anyone anything, yet he sees himself as a slave. What do you think St. Paul means by this statement?
- How is a slave for Christ different from a slave that does labor?
- St. Paul speaks of *being all things to all people.* What do you suppose he means by this?
- What are some creative ways someone your age can reach out to others?

Taking My Scripture Home

St. Paul speaks of his recompense or reward for preaching the gospel. What are some rewards or blessings that might come to people who live the gospel? What happens to the love we feel inside when we share it with others? What can you do today to share God's love with someone?

MARK 1:29–39

This passage gives us a glimpse into the daily life of Jesus. Along with worshiping at the synagogue, preaching, teaching, and healing, Jesus takes time to go off by himself to pray. The image of Jesus as the great healer seems to speak to the suffering expressed by Job in the first reading.

- What are some miraculous things Jesus did in this Gospel?
- Describe how you would feel if you were an eyewitness to these miracles.
- How do you suppose Jesus felt with an entire town waiting for him and watching his every move?
- What did Jesus have to do the next morning in order to find time to pray?
- Why do you think he went off by himself?
- What importance do you think prayer had in Jesus' life?
- Why is it important for people today to find time to pray?
- The Gospel says that people were looking for Jesus the next morning. Why do you suppose they wanted to find him?
- Although others needed Jesus, he did not let anything distract from his prayer time. What are some things that distract people from prayer time today?

Taking My Scripture Home

What are the major distractions in your day that keep you from quality prayer time? What can you do to make time in your day for prayer, even if it means getting up earlier in the morning?

Sixth Sunday of Ordinary Time

LEVITICUS 13:1–2, 44–46

The book of Leviticus contains 247 different laws that governed the everyday affairs of the Jewish people. Living under the law was a way for the Jewish people to express their dependence on God and rejoice in the special relationship they had with the Lord. This passage provides specific instructions on how to deal with leprosy.

- This passage speaks of how someone afflicted with leprosy must live. Why do you suppose it was important for the Jewish people to deal with leprosy in this way?
- What did someone with leprosy have to do according to these laws?
- What do you think were the concerns, fears, and feelings of those who had leprosy back in the time of Leviticus?
- How do you suppose those who had leprosy felt being forced to live outside of the community?
- Who are some people today that seem to be unwelcome in our communities?

Taking My Scripture Home

What are some unclean or unhealthy attitudes people have that adversely affect the rest of the community? Who are some of the people judged to be unclean in our society? How can you be welcoming to these people?

RESPONSORIAL PSALM REFLECTION: PSALM 32:7

- How do you turn to God?
- What are the things that trouble you and cause you to turn to God?
- When have you experienced the joy of salvation?

1 CORINTHIANS 10:31—11:1

At the time of this letter the people in the Corinthian church were from many different cultures and backgrounds. St. Paul pleads with the Corinthians to become united in Christ. He urges the Corinthians to be sensitive to the customs others hold closely and to seek the benefit of all people.

- St. Paul teaches the Corinthians to glorify God in all that they do. What does it mean to *glorify God?*
- How can our actions glorify God?
- What are some actions that do not glorify God?
- St. Paul also instructs the Corinthians to avoid offending others and to seek the benefit of others. Why do you suppose it is important to act in these ways toward others?
- What are some ways that people can act for the benefit of others?
- St. Paul urges the Corinthians to imitate Christ. What are some ways people imitate Christ in today's society?
- What are some ways one could imitate Christ at school or home?
- What qualities distinguish a person who imitates Christ from someone who does not live according to Christ's teachings?

Taking My Scripture Home

What are some ways you put your own benefit before that of others? What can you do this week to seek the benefit of others without considering your own benefit? What can you do to glorify God through your actions?

MARK 1:40—45

The first reading this Sunday from Leviticus provided insights into the difficult life of a leper. In this passage Jesus heals a leper and restores him to full life in the community. Despite stern warnings from Jesus, the leper was so filled with gratitude and excitement he could not contain the good news of his healing.

- The leper believed Jesus could heal him and begged for Jesus to do so. How do you suppose Jesus felt when he experienced this man's faith and situation?
- What do you think the healing meant to the leper?
- What are some ways people today may need spiritual healing?
- Besides being healed, the leper was now able to enter fully into the community again. How can the act of forgiveness have a similar effect on people today?
- Jesus told the healed leper to keep quiet about his healing, yet the man told the whole thing to everyone. Why would the healed leper have done this?

- How do you suppose people feel when they are forgiven from a serious offense?
- What are some of the teachings of Jesus that help heal and comfort people?

Taking My Scripture Home

Jesus in this Gospel reached out to a desperate leper and made him healthy again. Who are the desperate people in your life who are in need of someone to reach out to them? How can your actions or attitudes toward these people be a sign of God's loving and healing presence?

Seventh Sunday of Ordinary Time

ISAIAH 43:18–19, 21–22, 24b–25

This passage was written near the end of the Babylonian exile. The prophet describes a loving God who cares for the Israelites and forgives all their sins. He claims the Israelites no longer have to look back in their history to the time when Moses led them out of Egypt in order to find God's goodness. This release from Babylonian exile is every bit as wonderful as their release from Egypt. But it is God's mercy, not the Israelites' faithfulness, that wins their freedom.

- The author in this passage writes about how the Lord is doing something wonderful with the release of the Israelites from captivity in Babylonia. What are some ways sinfulness can be like a prison to people today?
- The author continues by citing ways the Lord helped the Israelites in the desert, yet they were sinful in return. What are some ways God shows love to us today?
- This passage continues with a description of how God forgave the sins of Israel. How do you feel knowing God is merciful?
- In your own life how do you feel when a family member or friend forgives you?
- What sacrament helps those who need to feel forgiven?

Taking My Scripture Home

Do you forgive others when they hurt you? How can God's example of radical forgiveness be an inspiration for your life?

RESPONSORIAL PSALM REFLECTION: PSALM 41:5b

- In what ways do we sin against God?
- What are the characteristics of a healthy soul?
- How can you let God heal your soul?

2 CORINTHIANS 1:18–22

St. Paul's second letter to the Corinthian church was written around AD 57, approximately one year after his first letter. In this passage St. Paul defends his indecisiveness about the timing of his return to the city of Corinth and pleads for the people of Corinth to focus on the promises of God.

- St. Paul speaks of the faithfulness of God. In today's society how do we experience God's faithfulness?
- St. Paul goes on to talk about God's promises. What are some of God's promises?
- How are the promises of God relevant for today's society?
- How can these promises bring people peace or security?
- Where do some people in today's society try to find peace and security?

Taking My Scripture Home

What are some ways God has been faithful to you? How can focusing on the promises of God bring you security each day?

MARK 2:1–12

This story is also recorded in the Gospels of Matthew and Luke. The authority of Jesus over sickness, forgiveness of sins, faithfulness of friends, and the continued disbelief of some are general themes of this amazing event.

- How do the friends feel about the paralytic?
- How do you think the paralytic felt when his friends displayed such determination to bring him to Jesus?
- How do you suppose Jesus felt when he witnessed the faith of the men?
- The paralytic was unable to bring himself to Jesus. In today's society who are those that are helpless?
- What obstacles stood in the way for the friends?
- What are some common obstacles that can be in our way when we try to help those who need it?
- In the story Jesus forgives the paralytic's sins. Why was forgiveness important?
- How can forgiving people help heal them?

Taking My Scripture Home

Who are those in today's society that need your help? What obstacles can you move to help them? Who do you know that needs your forgiveness?

Eighth Sunday of Ordinary Time

HOSEA 2:16b, 17b, 21–22

The book of Hosea was written around 730 BC. Hosea was a prophet who used his own marriage to an unfaithful wife as a symbolic example of the Israelites' unfaithfulness to God.

- Where does the Lord speak to the Israelites in this passage?
- Why do you suppose God chose a desert?
- Where do you go for quiet time with God?
- What are some distractions that keep people from spending quiet time with God?
- What does it mean to speak to someone's heart?

Taking My Scripture Home

How much quiet time do you spend with God? How can you become more open-hearted to God? What specific ways can you eliminate distractions that keep you from quiet time with God?

RESPONSORIAL PSALM REFLECTION: PSALM 103:8a

- Where have you seen God's kindness and mercy in your own life?
- How can you extend kindness and mercy to others?

2 CORINTHIANS 3:1b–6

In St. Paul's time there were preachers that took special pride in their written credentials. These preachers may well have questioned St. Paul's teaching because of his lack of such credentials. In this passage St. Paul defends himself by pointing out that the very existence of Christians in Corinth speaks of his credentials. These people and their faith were his letters of recommendation.

- In this passage St. Paul points out that people's actions show that they are Christians. What are some Christian actions?
- Where have you witnessed Christian actions in today's society?
- St. Paul speaks of letters that are written on people's hearts. What do you suppose this means?
- What is the difference between following rules and following your heart?
- How is being a Christian more than following rules?

Taking My Scripture Home

What Christian values and rules are written on your heart? How do your actions show God's love to others?

MARK 2:18–22

In this passage Jesus challenges the old way of time-honored traditions such as fasting. Jesus speaks of a new perspective, a perspective in which the relationship with God is based on love that governs the hearts and souls of people.

- The people in this passage have a difficult time understanding Jesus and the lack of respect for traditions he seems to exhibit. What is the difference between the laws of the Pharisees and the law that Jesus taught?
- What did Jesus teach?
- In the Gospel Jesus spoke of the dangers of mixing old cloth with new and new wine with old wineskins. What do you suppose Jesus was trying to say about a new way of relating to God?
- In the Gospel the people criticized Jesus' disciples for worshiping in an unconventional way. In today's society do you think people sometimes criticize others for worshiping in a dissimilar way? Explain.
- What are some reasons people should be tolerant of the way others worship?

Taking My Scripture Home

Are you critical or tolerant of other's religious traditions, culture, or lifestyle? Why are respect and tolerance for others important Christian values?

Tenth Sunday of Ordinary Time

(The Ninth Sunday of Ordinary Time is skipped in most Cycle Bs because of the length of Lent.)

GENESIS 3:9–15

This passage from Genesis captures Adam and Eve trying to shift the blame for their disobedience and God cursing the snake. To some the snake represents Satan, and the offspring who is to strike at the snake's head symbolizes Jesus. The snake being targeted in the head may be a prophetic reference to the eventual victory of life over death.

- Why do you suppose Adam was afraid of God in the garden and ashamed that he was naked?
- How might people today try to hide themselves from God?
- Both Adam and Eve blamed someone else for their actions. Why is it important to admit when we do something wrong?
- In today's society when have you seen someone try to blame another person for her or his own mistake?
- Eve told God the snake tricked her into eating the fruit. What are some excuses people use today for not following God?
- Instead of trusting God, Adam and Eve trusted the snake. What are some alluring things in our culture that might tempt us to trust in something besides God?

Taking My Scripture Home

Adam and Eve misplaced their trust. How can you make sure the people you trust are worthy of that trust? How much do you trust God? How can you deepen your dependence on God?

RESPONSORIAL PSALM REFLECTION: PSALM 130:7bc

- How do you feel knowing that the Lord is merciful?
- What does it mean to say there is fullness of redemption in the Lord?
- What areas of your life are in need of redemption?

2 CORINTHIANS 4:13—5:1

This passage is taken from a beautiful and moving portion of St. Paul's second letter to the Corinthians. St. Paul comforts the Corinthians as he speaks of how their afflictions produce a glory that lasts forever. He assures them that they, too, will share in the resurrection of Christ.

- How do you suppose the Corinthians felt when they read that St. Paul believes they will be raised from the dead and be together in God's presence?
- The author speaks of grace given in abundance so that our thanksgiving will glorify God. What do you think this means?
- St. Paul writes that our interior life is being renewed while our external life wastes away. What is he referring to here?
- What are some afflictions people might endure today that could produce glory for God?
- What are the unseen and eternal things that St. Paul is referring to in this passage?
- What do you think St. Paul meant by saying if our tent here on earth should be destroyed, God will provide us an eternal building in heaven?

Taking My Scripture Home

St. Paul comforts the Corinthians in this letter by challenging them to see beyond the physical to the eternal. How can these words help you expand your perspective? What are some ways God works through you? How do you feel knowing that you will be raised up to live in God's presence?

MARK 3:20—35

In this passage from Mark's Gospel the theme of battle between good and evil is resumed from the first reading. Here Jesus must defend his actions by explaining that it is in God's name that he casts out demons. He warns that it is blasphemous to call the Spirit of God unclean. In fact, those who live in the Spirit of God and do God's will are Jesus' brothers and sisters.

- Why do you suppose the scribes accused Jesus of being possessed by the devil?

- What are some examples of how people with good intentions might be misjudged today?
- Jesus used parables to explain that good and evil stand against each other. Where do you see this battle between good and evil taking place in the world today?
- What does it mean to blaspheme against the Holy Spirit?
- Why would Jesus have said that those who blaspheme against the Holy Spirit will never be forgiven?
- What do you think Jesus was implying about the battle of good and evil when he said those who do the will of God are his brothers and sisters?
- How can people show by their actions and attitudes that they have the Spirit of God within them?

Taking My Scripture Home

What can you do to strengthen your response to the Spirit of God's presence within you? How can you stand up to evil in your community and make a difference for good? When might you have an opportunity to respond to cruelty, hate, or prejudice in a way that exhibits patience, forgiveness, or kindness?

Eleventh Sunday of Ordinary Time

EZEKIEL 17:22–24

Ezekiel the prophet wrote from 593 BC to 571 BC and is often called the "Father of Judaism." Therefore, his influence can be found throughout the New Testament. In this passage he uses the image of a tree to speak of how God will restore Israel.

- Ezekiel uses symbolism as he writes about the Lord transplanting a shoot of cedar atop the mountain of Israel. What do you suppose the shoot of cedar represents?
- What is the significance of the Lord planting the cedar on the top of a mountain in Israel?
- Ezekiel continues by describing how the tree will flourish. What do you think this means?
- From Ezekiel's description of God, what can you tell about how Ezekiel perceived God?
- Where have you seen God's amazing power and greatness displayed?
- What are some ways God renews and restores those who believe?

Taking My Scripture Home

Ezekiel uses vivid images to capture God's power and strength. What are some images you have of God? How does God's strength bring forth life in the people who believe?

RESPONSORIAL PSALM REFLECTION: PSALM 92:2a

- Why is it good to give thanks to God?
- What happens inside a person who reflects upon the goodness of God?
- How does a person filled with gratitude act?

2 CORINTHIANS 5:6–10

In this passage St. Paul encourages the Corinthians to continue as disciples of Christ and strive to please God even though they cannot physically see God. The time in our physical bodies is only temporary.

- What does St. Paul mean by saying that we are away from God while we are in our bodies?
- What does it mean to *walk by faith and not by sight?*
- What are some examples of how people walk by faith?
- Why do you suppose St. Paul called Christians courageous?
- What are some ways you have seen Christians be courageous?
- Why do you suppose the audience of this letter would rather be home with the Lord than living in their bodies?
- Do you think this is the viewpoint of most people in today's society? Why or why not?
- Why do you think people today fear death?
- How do you feel knowing Christ will judge you?
- What do you know about God that gives you insight into what it will be like to meet God face to face?

Taking My Scripture Home

What are ways that you can be more courageous in your faith? How can knowing God loves you unconditionally give you energy and strength to extend God's love to others?

MARK 4:26–34

In this passage Jesus uses symbolism that common people of that time would understand. Plants are used once again to communicate something about the kingdom of God. The mysterious growth of plants speaks of how God's plan is beyond our understanding yet it unfolds gradually. The image of the great plant sprouting from the mustard seed reveals how God's kingdom will be far-reaching and provide life for all.

- How would you explain the parable of scattered seed that grows into plants?
- What are some mysteries of God that we do not understand?
- Why do you suppose Jesus used parables and stories to explain things to the crowds?
- How would you explain the second parable about the mustard seed growing into a life-giving plant?
- How do you feel knowing God's love is meant for all people?
- Where in your life have you experienced God's life-giving power?
- How can you become more life-giving in your attitudes and actions?

Taking My Scripture Home

What can you do to nurture the seed of God's love in your own heart? What would happen in your own life if God's love were to flourish like a huge plant?

Twelfth Sunday of Ordinary Time

JOB 38:1, 8–11

The book of Job is the story of a godly man, Job, who goes through great losses: loss of wealth, family, and health. His friends encourage him to curse God. Instead, Job asks God for an explanation. God responds and reminds Job of the extent of God's power. This passage is a part of God's response.

- The first few lines of this reading ask a question. What is the answer to the question?
- What do you suppose the author was trying to convey in this story?
- This reading speaks of God's power and vastness. In your own life where have you seen the power or vastness of God?
- How do you think people would feel if they realized such a powerful God loves them unconditionally?
- How should we respond to such love?

Taking My Scripture Home

When have you experienced God's great love? How can you open your heart to God each day?

RESPONSORIAL PSALM REFLECTION: PSALM 107:1b

- Why would you like to give thanks to the Lord?
- What does *everlasting* mean?
- Do you think God's love is everlasting even when we sin? Explain.

2 CORINTHIANS 5:14–17

In this passage St. Paul speaks of how Christians participate in a new creation in Christ. This new creation is not found in the physical world, but is a participation in the resurrection of Jesus. Living for others and not for oneself is the sign of this new creation.

- What does the word *impel* mean?
- Why would Christ's love impel us to action?
- In today's society what types of things motivate people to action?
- What are some things that Christians do because of Christ's great love?
- St. Paul speaks of how those who are in Christ are a new creation. What does it mean to be *in Christ?*
- Why would Christians be a new creation?
- What types of habits, desires, or tendencies would a Christian relinquish?

Taking My Scripture Home

Do you really believe in Christ's love? How can that great love move you to action? How are you a new creation because of that love?

MARK 4:35–41

This passage gives us a glimpse of Jesus' power over nature. The event is also recorded in Matthew's Gospel. This amazing miracle was a sign to help build the disciples' faith.

- How do you think the disciples felt before waking Jesus?
- What are some things in today's society that are frightening?
- The disciples were worried about the storm. What are some things that people your age worry about today?
- What did the disciples do when they were worried?
- What are some things people your age do when they are worried?
- What are some Christian responses to worry?
- Jesus calmed the storm. How is this theme similar to the one in the first reading?
- What are some ways people respond to the power and awe of God?

Taking My Scripture Home

What are some of your worries? When can you schedule time each day to talk with God about your worries and concerns? How can you believe more fully in the power of God?

Thirteenth Sunday of Ordinary Time

WISDOM 1:13–15; 2:23–24

The book of Wisdom is attributed to Solomon, although it was written after his death. It was designed to educate the Jewish people and give them comfort during a time of oppression. This book is not found in the Protestant Bible.

- Is it obvious that God did not make death, or do some people blame the Lord for suffering and death? Explain.
- Why do you suppose some people blame God for misfortune?
- What does it mean to say *the creatures of the world are wholesome?*
- How can you tell if someone truly believes people and creation are good?
- How do you feel knowing God created you and others to be imperishable?
- How does the devil's envy cause suffering and death?
- What are some ways we can choose to belong to the company of God instead of the company of the devil?

Taking My Scripture Home

How do you feel knowing you are created in God's own image? When have you felt God's goodness within you? How can you share the goodness within yourself with others?

RESPONSORIAL PSALM REFLECTION: PSALM 30:2a

- How can your attitudes and actions praise God?
- In what ways has the Lord rescued you?
- How does praising God create joy and peace within people?

2 CORINTHIANS 8:7, 9, 13–15

St. Paul eloquently makes the case for equality and charity in this passage. The passage that he cites is from the experience the Israelites had when gathering manna in the desert. God treated all as equal.

- What are some examples of how people today can excel in graciousness?
- Why do you suppose equality was important to St. Paul?
- St. Paul describes how Jesus abandoned richness so that others might be rich. What do you suppose he means by this?
- What are some other ways God's generosity is shown to us?
- St. Paul urges the Corinthians to share their abundance so that the needs of all are met. How well does our society share their abundance with others?
- Why should all people be treated with equality?
- Why do you think it is difficult for some people to share their abundance with others?
- Other than material belongings, what else can you share generously with others?

Taking My Scripture Home

When have you experienced generosity from someone? How did you feel when someone extended generosity to you? What power do you have to create good will and love among others with the abundance you have been given?

MARK 5:21–43

Two amazing miracles are interwoven in this passage. In both cases Jesus was able to do remarkable things because of the faith of the father and the faith of the hemorrhaging woman. Each of these people believed that a mere touch from Jesus was enough to heal. This faith was a far cry from the disbelief of those who ridiculed Jesus for announcing the child was asleep.

- What did the father's words to Jesus reveal about his faith in Jesus?
- Why do you suppose both the hemorrhaging woman and the father had so much faith in the touch of Jesus?
- What role did their faith play in the healings?
- How does Jesus' message of forgiveness and love help create healing among people today?
- How can we act in healing ways toward others?
- How do people today show their faith in God?
- Why do you suppose Jesus put out those who ridiculed him for saying the girl was asleep?
- How can our faith or lack of faith affect others?

Taking My Scripture Home

Have you ever considered how your faith might affect others? How can your enthusiasm for God's Word be a healing presence to other people? When have you experienced God's healing and how can you let that experience fill you with gratitude and awe?

Fourteenth Sunday of Ordinary Time

EZEKIEL 2:2–5

This passage is the story of God's call to Ezekiel to become a prophet. God makes it clear to Ezekiel that being a prophet would not be an easy calling. Ezekiel was instructed to speak in the Lord's name so that all would know a prophet was in their presence.

- To whom was God sending Ezekiel?
- Why was Ezekiel sent?
- Do you see rebellion against God in today's society? Explain.
- God tells Ezekiel that the Israelites might not listen to him, yet, they will know he had been sent by God. How do people today seem to ignore God's Word?
- How do people know if there is a Christian in their presence?
- What are some ways Christians can communicate their love for God without saying anything?

Taking My Scripture Home

Do others know that a Christian is among them when you are in their presence? What types of actions can you take to make others sense God's presence in you?

RESPONSORIAL PSALM REFLECTION: PSALM 123:2cd

- What does it mean to fix your eyes on something?
- What are some characteristics of those who are focused on God?
- How do people receive God's mercy?

2 CORINTHIANS 12:7–10

This well-known passage speaks of "a thorn in the flesh," something that is a bother to St. Paul. While it is unclear what this affliction might be, the point seems to be that even in his suffering St. Paul sees the glory of God.

- What do you think the *thorn* might be?
- How does this affliction make St. Paul dependent on God?
- What are some afflictions people today might face?
- How can dependence on God help people with their afflictions?
- How can there be strength in weakness?
- How does today's society feel about weakness?
- Who are some people that appear to be weak by society's standards but are strong in their Christian values, beliefs, and actions?
- How can those, such as Mother Teresa, be an example for us?

Taking My Scripture Home

What is *your* thorn? How can this affliction strengthen you as a Christian? How can you remember to depend on God when you are going through difficult times?

MARK 6:1–6

This event in Jesus' life shows the rejection of Jesus by his hometown people in Nazareth. Also shown in this passage is the lack of faith by the people and how faith is needed before miracles can be performed.

- In the reading people were amazed, yet they did not believe. What are some ways people today experience God's amazing power?
- Why do you suppose people can experience everyday miracles and still not believe in God?
- Do you think people take everyday miracles for granted? Explain.
- Name some everyday miracles.
- The townspeople felt they knew Jesus and could not believe in his wisdom. What are some ways we overlook the wisdom of the people closest to us?
- Are there wise people in the world today that are not acknowledged? Explain.
- Why do you think Jesus was not able to perform miracles in his hometown?
- Why is having an open heart and faith important for experiencing God's love?
- The people had no faith in Jesus because they were too familiar with him. What are some ways relationships are hurt because people take each other for granted or become blinded to each other's mystery and uniqueness?

Taking My Scripture Home

How can opening your heart to God help you grow in your faith? What everyday miracles do you take for granted? Who are the people close to you that you take for granted?

Fifteenth Sunday of Ordinary Time

AMOS 7:12–15

Amos was a shepherd who was called to prophesy by God. Amos's prophecies were candid and straightforward, and often his audience did not receive them well. In this passage Amos has just spoken against a great king, and the priest who works for the king is angry.

- In this passage Amaziah is angry because Amos has spoken against the king, to whom Amaziah is loyal. What does Amaziah tell Amos to do?
- Why do you think Amaziah wanted Amos to leave?
- In today's society what are some ways people tune out the Word of God?
- Amos responds by telling Amaziah that he was simply called by God to speak God's Word. Who are some ordinary people you know that speak God's Word?
- How are Christians called to be prophets?
- What do you suppose God would want people to know today?

Taking My Scripture Home

What are some ways you tune out God's Word? How are you called to communicate God's Word to others?

RESPONSORIAL PSALM REFLECTION: PSALM 85:8

- Where do you see the Lord's kindness?
- How can you reflect that kindness to others?
- What is salvation? What are we saved from?

EPHESIANS 1:3—14

This passage, at the beginning of the book of Ephesians, is the greeting to the audience. The author emphasizes that we are blessed and chosen by God. We also have many blessings given to us by God. This letter was probably passed to many Gentile churches throughout the region.

- What do you suppose it means to be blessed in Christ?
- What are some spiritual blessings that you see in today's society?
- What does it mean to be chosen by God?
- What are some responsibilities that go along with being chosen by God?
- Why do you think the author expressed to the Gentile churches that they were chosen?
- List some of the blessings of God in this passage.
- Why do you suppose the author took so much time and space to list these blessings?

Taking My Scripture Home

How have you been blessed in Christ? In what specific ways can you utilize these blessings to bring God's love to others? For what purpose have you been chosen by God?

MARK 6:7—13

This passage recounts Jesus' instructions as he sent forth his disciples to preach the gospel. The disciples had witnessed Jesus' many wonderful actions and heard his teaching. Now they were called to act on what they had witnessed by going forth and preaching. Traveling light and making themselves vulnerable to the good will of those they met, the disciples would show their dependence on God.

- Why do you suppose the disciples were sent in pairs?
- Name the items the disciples were to take with them.
- How do you suppose the disciples felt when they were instructed to travel with just a few personal items?
- How did traveling with such few resources force the disciples to trust in God and the goodness of the people they met?
- How do you suppose these actions affected those who met the disciples as they preached?
- What are some luxuries that people today seem to think are necessities?
- What did Jesus instruct the disciples to do if they were not welcomed?
- How would the world be different today if people simply shook dust from their feet when they faced rejection or anger?
- Why do you think Jesus instructed the disciples in this nonviolent act?
- Do you think the disciples were successful in their mission? Explain.

Taking My Scripture Home

How do you handle anger or face rejection? How can you learn to handle feelings of resentment in a nonviolent manner? What mission could you be called to accomplish?

Sixteenth Sunday of Ordinary Time

JEREMIAH 23:1—6

Born in 650 BC, the prophet Jeremiah lived in a tumultuous time for the Israelites. During his lifetime the Jewish people lost their good king, Josiah, in battle to the Egyptians. After his death the people turned to idolatry, which Jeremiah opposed. Under Babylonian rule the Jewish people rebelled. In retaliation the Babylonians destroyed Jerusalem. Jeremiah later died in exile in Egypt.

- Jeremiah begins this passage with a warning to the shepherds who misled the Israelites. Why is good leadership so important?
- What are some examples of how leaders have hurt people?
- What are qualities of a good leader?
- How can good leaders bring blessings to people?
- How can people your age show leadership qualities?
- Jeremiah speaks of how God will appoint good shepherds to lead the Jewish people. How do you suppose Jesus fit this role of a good shepherd?

Taking My Scripture Home

What are some ways your actions and attitudes influence others? How can you make sure your actions and attitudes lead people to God? What prayers and support do your parents, teachers, coaches, principals, and political leaders need?

RESPONSORIAL PSALM REFLECTION: PSALM 23:1

- What does it mean to say *the Lord is my shepherd?*
- Why is there nothing you will want if the Lord is your shepherd?
- How does the Lord provide for you and others?

EPHESIANS 2:13–18

While St. Paul's comments in this passage are addressed to the Gentiles (non-Jewish people) of Ephesus, his words have relevance for people of all times and cultures. He speaks of how Christ rose above religious barriers to unite everyone through the blood of his cross.

- St. Paul speaks of how Christ reached out to those who were far away. What are some examples of how people today might be considered to be living far away from Christ?
- How does God's church reach out to people of diverse backgrounds today?
- How does Jesus' teachings abolish the old laws and commandments?
- What is the new law that Christ has written on our hearts?
- How does Christ's love unite people?
- What are some ways God's love brings peace into the world?
- How did Jesus bring people closer to God?

Taking My Scripture Home

What are some ways you can reach out with compassion to those who may be different from you? How can you strengthen your commitment to God's law of love?

MARK 6:30–34

This passage captures Jesus' tender and compassionate side as he feels pity for the crowds who hunger for food and spiritual nourishment. The image of the good shepherd is fitting, as Jesus is consumed with the well-being of the many instead of his own need for rest and food.

- What did Jesus and the disciples need at this time?
- Why do you suppose Jesus and the disciples went away to an isolated place in order to rest?
- How do you feel when you are very tired, yet you must deal with many people or responsibilities?
- How did Jesus respond when the crowds approached him?
- What can you tell about Jesus' character by the way he responded in this situation?
- When is it most difficult for people to act with patience?
- What is the secret to feeling compassion and patience for those in need?

Taking My Scripture Home

Who are the people in your world who hunger for friendship, affirmation, recognition, and trust? How can you open your heart to their needs? What are some ways people have expressed concern and respect for you?

Seventeenth Sunday of Ordinary Time

2 KINGS 4:42–44

The Lord was able to work through Elisha and the generosity of the man from Baal-shalishah to make a little food feed a large crowd. Later, Jesus was able to do the same thing when a boy shared his loaves and fish with a large crowd. In both stories a little generosity touches many people.

- Why do you suppose the man from Baal-shalishah gave Elisha the food?
- What are some examples of generosity that you have experienced?
- What did Elisha do with the food?
- Why do you suppose Elisha's servant objected to Elisha giving the food to the crowd?
- Why did Elisha feel confident the food would be enough to feed the crowd?
- What are some ways people today show they have confidence in the Lord's goodness?
- How can a person's generosity be used to touch many people today?

Taking My Scripture Home

What can you do to open yourself more generously to the needs of others? What are some things people your age might need besides food and drink? How can your concern and compassion make a difference with these people?

RESPONSORIAL PSALM REFLECTION: PSALM 145:16

- What are some things that we hunger for?
- How does the Lord feed us?
- What does God's willingness to meet our needs say about God?

EPHESIANS 4:1–6

This letter was written by St. Paul while he was in captivity, around AD 62. The letter may have been written as a circular letter, that is, it was taken to many different Christian communities and read to the people. The major theme of this letter and this passage is the unity of the church.

- What do you suppose is meant by preserving the unity of the church in this passage?
- How do peace, gentleness, and humility help unite people?
- What are some actions and attitudes that destroy unity?
- Why do you suppose unity is important?
- What can Christians do to reach out to those who do not experience unity with the Church?
- How might you expect people to act if they truly believed they were united with others?

Taking My Scripture Home

What can you do to let the spirit of humility, gentleness, and patience grow within you? What are some ways you can act to help bring about peace among people?

JOHN 6:1–15

Reminiscent of Elisha's story in the first reading, this passage shows Jesus feeding over five thousand people through the generosity of one boy. This amazing miracle not only satisfied the people's hunger, but also acted as a sign to build their faith. Unfortunately, many in the crowd missed the point, forcing Jesus to withdraw to avoid being made their king.

- Why was the crowd following Jesus in this story?
- How do you suppose the people felt when they witnessed this amazing miracle?
- In this story people were left in awe by the power Jesus possessed. What are some other qualities of God that leave us in awe?
- The loaves and fishes were able to satisfy the hunger of those in the crowd. What are other types of hungers that Jesus' teachings and actions are able to satisfy?
- Why do you suppose the people wanted to make Jesus their king after witnessing this miracle?
- Why do you think Jesus refused to become their king?
- What did this action say about Jesus' goals and values?
- This miracle was a sign of Jesus' goodness and power, one that the people could taste. What are some signs of God's love and mercy that people can feel in their hearts today?

Taking My Scripture Home

Why is it good to reflect on the goodness and power of God? How can you increase your trust in God and let God's Spirit feed your soul? How can you make the teachings of Jesus rule your life?

Eighteenth Sunday of Ordinary Time

EXODUS 16:2–4, 12–15

After the Israelites fled Egypt, they grew hungry in the desert and complained to Moses. The Lord, in response to their cries, provided bread from heaven, called "manna." The Jewish people ate this manna for forty years while in the desert. It became a symbol of how the Lord nourished the Israelites and called them into increasing dependence on God.

- The Lord saw that the Israelites were in need of food and God provided for them. What does this tell you about God?
- What are some needs people your age might have?
- How can we pray to God to provide for our needs?
- What part of the Lord's Prayer is a request that God provide for our daily needs?
- How do you suppose the Israelites responded to this manna that God provided for them?
- What are some ways people can become more dependent on the Lord today?

Taking My Scripture Home

How does the Lord provide for your needs today? How often do you recognize what God has provided for you? Do you remember to thank God for providing so much for you?

RESPONSORIAL PSALM REFLECTION: PSALM 78:24b

- What is implied about a God who would rain down bread from heaven?
- What are some other ways God provides for people?
- What are some ways you can pass along God's generosity to others?

EPHESIANS 4:17, 20–24

St. Paul in this passage speaks of how life as a Christian is a new existence and a different way of living. This conversion calls the Christian to abandon ways of corruption and deceit and replace these with purity of heart and truth. This interior conversion is a sign of one's new life in Christ.

- What does the word *futility* mean?
- St. Paul urges the people not to live in the futility of the Gentiles. What do you suppose he meant by this?
- What are some examples of how people live futile lives today?
- What are some examples of how people might live in corruption or deceit?
- How does a person turn away from corruption, deceit, or other selfish ways?
- In society today where do you find corruption, deceit, or selfish ways?
- St. Paul speaks of how Christians are created in God's way. What do you suppose helps Christians become formed more in God's way?

Taking My Scripture Home

These words from St. Paul's letter can be very challenging to us. What areas of your life belong to the old self? What areas of your life should be renewed in the Spirit?

JOHN 6:24–35

This passage builds on the manna theme introduced in the first reading. Here, Jesus identifies himself as the bread of life, a type of new manna that feeds the souls of those who believe. In this way Jesus is seen as a fulfillment of God's goodness that was extended to the Israelites in the desert.

- When the people came to Jesus in boats, what were they most interested in getting from him?
- What are some mistaken expectations or understandings of Jesus that people today might have?
- Jesus told the people not to work for food that is temporary, but to work, instead, for spiritual food that brings everlasting life. How would you describe this type of food?
- What are some values and priorities you might expect from someone who sincerely seeks the bread of life?
- When the people asked Jesus for a sign such as the manna given by Moses, Jesus responded by saying he is the bread of life. What significance do you suppose this had for the Jewish people in the crowd?
- What do you think Jesus meant by saying those who come to him will never hunger or thirst?

- What are some ways Jesus' teachings nourish our souls?
- In what ways does God sustain us both physically and spiritually?

Taking My Scripture Home

What are some ways God's love has made a difference in your life? How do you hunger and thirst for God's love? What can you do to increase your desire to become closer to God?

Nineteenth Sunday of Ordinary Time

1 KINGS 19:4—8

The prophet Elijah was on the run in this passage. King Ahab had turned from the Lord and worshiped Baal, one of the pagan gods. He was hunting down the prophets of the Lord and killing them. Elijah, however, had just demonstrated the Lord's superiority over Baal in front of the people of Israel. Afterward, Elijah killed 450 of the prophets of Baal. For these reasons Jezebel, Ahab's wife, promised to kill Elijah. The Lord's nourishment gave Elijah amazing strength to survive this struggle.

- Elijah was so distraught that he prayed for death. What are some struggles people face today that make it very difficult for them to go on?
- Did the Lord grant Elijah his wish and end his life? What did God do instead?
- Why do you suppose God did not allow Elijah to die?
- How does the Lord provide for people today?
- Elijah was able to walk for forty days and nights because of the strength provided by the angel's food. How does our hope in God give us strength to endure hardships in our lives?
- What do the angel's food and drink symbolically represent?

Taking My Scripture Home

How does the Lord provide for your needs? Elijah had amazing endurance after eating the food provided by the Lord. How does God's love give you energy and enthusiasm to help others?

RESPONSORIAL PSALM REFLECTION: PSALM 34:9a

- What are some ways you have experienced the Lord's goodness?
- What effect does God's goodness have on you?
- How can you reflect God's goodness to others?

EPHESIANS 4:30—5:2

In this passage St. Paul encourages the people to purify their hearts and put aside worldly ways. He speaks of how Christians should imitate Christ and live in the spirit of love.

- St. Paul tells the people not to grieve the Holy Spirit. What do you suppose this means?
- What are some examples of behavior, values, or attitudes that are inconsistent with Christian values?
- How does a person change impure behaviors, values, or attitudes?
- What happens to a community when people act with kindness, compassion, and forgiveness?
- What does it mean to imitate God and to live in love?
- Who are some people you know that seem to live in God's love?

Taking My Scripture Home

When is it especially easy for you to live in God's love? When is it especially difficult for you to live in God's love? What can you do to let God's love have a stronger control over your life?

JOHN 6:41–51

The Jews who knew Jesus' parents could not understand why Jesus referred to himself as the bread from heaven. In response Jesus elaborated on how he is the bread of life and those who believe in him will never die.

- Why do you suppose the Jews who knew Jesus' parents had such trouble accepting that he was the bread of life?
- How can our familiarity with family and friends make it difficult at times to see their goodness?
- Jesus speaks of how those who listen to the Father come to him. What were some messages about God that Jesus brought to the people?
- What benefits and value does food have for people today?
- What do you suppose was implied when Jesus referred to himself as the bread of life?
- What do you think Jesus meant when he said those who eat this bread will never die?

- Where in your life have you experienced love, kindness, support, and nourishment?
- Why do you suppose God's love is stronger than sin and death?

Taking My Scripture Home

How do you feel knowing God is always with you? Which passages from Scripture give you strength in times of trouble? God's energy and strength will never die. When in your life have you experienced this energy and strength from God?

Twentieth Sunday of Ordinary Time

PROVERBS 9:1–6

The book of Proverbs is a collection of poetry designed to teach wisdom. An unknown religious sage wrote this passage sometime in the fifth century BC. Here the author describes wisdom as a matron who provides life-giving food for the spiritual journey.

- The author speaks of Wisdom as a woman. In reality what is wisdom?
- Where does wisdom come from?
- This passage says Wisdom sends out maidens to call people to her feast. What do you suppose the author is trying to say about God's desire to reach out to people?
- How does the Lord invite people today to turn from foolishness and embrace God's wisdom?
- What actions or attitudes would you expect to find in someone who is filled with God's wisdom?
- What actions or attitudes would you expect to find in someone who turns his or her back on God's wisdom?
- How does God's wisdom bring goodness, peace, and life into the world?

Taking My Scripture Home

How can you increase your understanding of God's wisdom? How can God's wisdom help bring peace to a stressed relationship in your life?

RESPONSORIAL PSALM REFLECTION: PSALM 34:9a

- How does the Lord's goodness nourish you?
- How can you sense God's goodness in your life?
- In whom have you experienced God's goodness?

EPHESIANS 5:15–20

Building on the wisdom theme introduced in the first reading, this passage from Ephesians implores the people to take initiative and become knowledgeable about what pleases God. Similar words are written in the letter to the Colossians.

- The author speaks of watching carefully how we live. Why is it important to pay attention to how we live?
- What are some examples of how lifestyles in our culture reflect the values people have?
- What are some practices in our culture that are not based on God's message of love?
- What are some lifestyle choices people make that show they truly desire to live according to God's will?
- The author provides a wonderful image of those whose hearts are filled with God's Spirit. How can God's Spirit affect our actions?
- Why is it important for us to be grateful to God?
- How do a person's actions and words show that he or she is grateful for God's goodness?

Taking My Scripture Home

What can you do to increase your knowledge of God's will? What choices can you make this week that will reflect your desire to do God's will?

JOHN 6:51–58

This passage continues the story that began on the Seventeenth Sunday of Ordinary Time. Early in the Gospel, Jesus had multiplied the loaves and fed the crowd. The crowd then followed Jesus to Capernaum where this discourse is recorded.

- The Jews had trouble understanding what Jesus meant when he offered his flesh as food. What do you suppose Jesus meant by this?
- Besides receiving the Eucharist, what are some other ways people might be nourished by Jesus?
- What might be the difference between someone who casually listens to Jesus' message and someone who truly lets Jesus' message become a part of him or her?

- How do people let God's Word become a part of their lives?
- How would the world be different if everyone truly fed on the Word of God?
- Jesus said those who do not eat his flesh do not have life within them. What are some things people might value above God's Word?

Taking My Scripture Home

Jesus challenges us to make his Word a real part of our lives. What can you do to deepen your dependence on God? How can you recommit yourself to God's Word?

Twenty-first Sunday of Ordinary Time

JOSHUA 24:1—2a, 15—17, 18b

Joshua was the leader of the Israelite people who brought them into the Promised Land after Moses died. In this passage Joshua is addressing the Israelites as an old man, leaving them with a message before his death.

- Why do you think Joshua gathered all the people together for his message?
- What choices did Joshua give the people regarding whom to worship?
- What are some things, other than God, that people worship today?
- How can you tell if a household serves the Lord?
- After Joshua's question the Israelites remembered all that God did for them during their journey. What are some ways God takes care of people today?

Taking My Scripture Home

Can others tell that you serve the Lord? What are some ways you can make your service to God abundantly clear to others? How does God take care of you?

RESPONSORIAL PSALM REFLECTION: PSALM 34:9a

- How is the Lord good?
- What are some ways people miss God's goodness?
- Why is it important to make a point to look for and enjoy God's goodness?

EPHESIANS 5:21–32

In this passage St. Paul uses common relationships to illustrate the relationship of Christ and the Church. In St. Paul's time wives were not always treated well or with respect. Often they were regarded as property. In urging all to be subordinate to one another, St. Paul repeats Jesus' message to love and respect all people regardless of social status.

- What are some characteristics of a relationship in which two people are subordinate to one another?
- Why is it important to attempt to have this type of relationship with everyone?
- In St. Paul's time husbands were given a higher status than wives. Who in our society enjoys high status?
- Who has a low status in our society?
- St. Paul urges husbands to love their wives. Whom would St. Paul urge our society to love today?
- How does Christ cherish and nourish the Church?
- What are the similarities between married love and God's love for the Church?

Taking My Scripture Home

Whom do you need to love regardless of status? How can Christ's example of love and nourishment be a model for you to follow?

JOHN 6:60–69

This passage comes at the end of Jesus' Bread of Life discourse. This message was quite unusual and very radical. These words give us insight into how the message was received.

- The disciples complained that Jesus' message was hard to accept. What things do people have a hard time accepting about Jesus' message today?
- What do you suppose Jesus meant when he said that his words were *Spirit and life?*
- Why do you think some disciples did not believe and returned home?
- Who was the one who would betray Jesus?
- What did Simon Peter say to Jesus?
- How can our faith change us so there is no going back to a former way of life?

Taking My Scripture Home

What is the hardest thing for you to accept about Jesus' message? What can you do to recommit yourself to God and let God's love work through you?

Twenty-second Sunday of Ordinary Time

DEUTERONOMY 4:1–2, 6–8

Deuteronomy is the fifth book of the Old Testament. It was written to remind the Israelites of their covenant with God. In keeping the laws given to them by God, they were identified with God and recognized as God's own people.

- Why do you suppose the Israelites needed a set of statutes, laws, and decrees to follow?
- What are some laws of God that we follow today?
- Why does following God's laws show wisdom?
- Moses tells the people that other nations will look at them and describe them as a great nation. Why would following God's laws make them a great nation?
- What activities or actions would you expect from a nation that followed God's laws?
- Which of God's laws do you feel people or nations find difficult to follow today?
- Why would following God's laws keep the Israelites close to God?

Taking My Scripture Home

Which of God's laws do you have a difficult time following? What can you do to make a concentrated effort to follow those laws? What actions or activities would bring you closer to God?

RESPONSORIAL PSALM REFLECTION: PSALM 15:1a

- What does it mean to *do* justice?
- What specific actions would a just person do?
- Why would those who are just be close to God?

JAMES 1:17–18, 21b–22, 27

It is unclear who the author of the book of James is or when it was written. Some experts believe it was written around AD 52 and that the author was James, a relative of Jesus. Others believe it was written much later by one of the followers of James. In either case the author of James wrote for an early Jewish Christian community and his letter focused on living morally.

- The author speaks of God as the *Father of lights*. What does this image bring to mind?
- Do you think this is an accurate description of God? Explain.
- How does one *humbly welcome the word?*
- What are some other options when we hear God's Word?
- Describe someone who is a *doer*.
- How would that person be different than a *hearer* only?
- The author of James urges the audience to remain unstained by the world. How do you think the world can stain us?
- Describe a typical teenager today who is stained by the world.
- What specific ways can people keep themselves from being stained?

Taking My Scripture Home

Are you a doer of the Word? What actions show that you are a doer? How can you remain unstained by today's society?

MARK 7:1–8, 14–15, 21–23

There were numerous laws, customs, and traditions about purification and washing dating back to the time of Moses. The Pharisees were a group of well-educated Jews who were meticulous in following all the Jewish laws and customs. Scribes were also well educated in the law of Moses.

- What motive prompted the scribes and Pharisees to ask Jesus why his disciples did not wash before eating?
- Why would Jesus call them hypocrites?
- What do you suppose is hypocritical about performing religious acts while one's heart is not open to God?
- Do you think there are hypocrites in today's society? Explain.
- What are characteristics of someone who is not hypocritical?
- Jesus told the Pharisees that they disregard God's commandment. What commandment do you think Jesus was talking about?
- What does the word *defile* mean?
- How could thoughts and feelings defile people?

Taking My Scripture Home

When have your motives not been pure? What are some ways you can keep your heart undefiled? How can God's commandment of love be the motive for your thoughts and actions?

Twenty-third Sunday of Ordinary Time

ISAIAH 35:4–7a

This passage from Isaiah looks forward to a time when the tribes of Israel are brought together and Jerusalem is restored. The imagery of the blind, deaf, and lame being healed is reminiscent of the healing works Jesus was to perform later.

- The author encourages the people not to be afraid. What do you suppose may have frightened the people?
- God is described as coming with vindication (forgiveness) and wanting to save the people. How did this prediction come true through Jesus?
- What effect do you suppose God's willingness to forgive and save the people might have had upon the Israelites at the time?
- What are some of the wonderful things the author says will happen when the Lord saves the people?
- What are some wonderful transformations that happen to people when God's Spirit enters into their lives?
- How can God's love transform an entire community or town?

Taking My Scripture Home

The author of Isaiah comforted the people by describing God not as harsh and judging, but as forgiving and willing to save. What are some ways you can imitate these qualities of God in your life? How can your actions help transform the people around you?

RESPONSORIAL PSALM REFLECTION: PSALM 146:1b

- How can you praise the Lord?
- Why is God worthy of praise?
- How can you always keep God's praises in your soul?

JAMES 2:1–5

The author of James continues his letter to early Christians with guidance on living morally. The challenge not to show favoritism to the rich and discriminate against the poor is reminiscent of the early Church described in Acts.

- What are some ways people today discriminate against others based on their appearance?
- How do you suppose it feels to be treated badly because of poverty?
- Why is it wrong to judge others based on their material wealth?
- What sort of motives might be behind the intentions of those who show undue favor to the rich?
- What can people do to become more accepting of and open to others?
- Why would the poor be chosen to be rich in faith?

Taking My Scripture Home

What are some ways you may have judged others based on their appearance? How can you grow in your ability to see the goodness in all people, regardless of their social status? How do you feel when you yourself have been judged harshly?

MARK 7:31–37

Jesus restoring hearing to the deaf and making the mute speak sounds much like the fulfillment of Isaiah's prophecy in the first reading. The people who witnessed this miracle were so filled with amazement that they told everyone, despite Jesus' orders not to tell anyone.

- Those who brought the deaf and mute man begged Jesus to touch him. What do you suppose this action revealed about their faith in Jesus?
- Why do you suppose Jesus took the man away from the crowds?
- How do you think the man felt when he was healed?
- What are some ways God's forgiveness and love help make people feel healed today?
- Why do you suppose the people who witnessed this miracle told everyone despite Jesus' protests?

- The Psalm response speaks of praising the Lord. Would you consider the people who spoke of this miracle to be praising God? Explain.
- What are some reasons people today could be filled with praise for God?

Taking My Scripture Home

How does God's love touch you? Who are the people in your life through whom God's love has reached you? Remembering the times in your life when you felt God's presence most strongly, how did you praise God?

Twenty-fourth Sunday of Ordinary Time

ISAIAH 50:4c—9a

The book of Isaiah contains four different prophecies about the servant of the Lord. This passage is the third of these prophecies. In it the servant of the Lord is speaking. These words offer encouragement and hope to all who serve the Lord.

- How would you describe the way the servant is treated in the first part of this passage?
- What are some hardships people your age might encounter as they try to live their faith?
- The tone changes in the second part of this passage. How would you describe the servant's response to the suffering he or she must endure?
- How can our faith help us endure suffering and hard times?
- Why do you suppose the servant has so much confidence in God's help?
- What are some ways people today show their confidence in God's love?

Taking My Scripture Home

What sacrifices or hardships have you had to face in your life? How does God's love sustain you in these times? How can these struggles bring you closer to God?

RESPONSORIAL PSALM REFLECTION: PSALM 116:9

- What does it mean to *walk before the Lord?*
- What images come to mind when you think of *the land of the living?*
- How does God's presence bring joy into our lives?

JAMES 2:14–18

The author of James continues the practical advice to early Christians on how to live a moral, Christian life. In this passage the author stresses the importance of both good works and faith.

- The author of James speaks of the importance of acting with love. In your opinion is it easier for a person to claim to have faith, or to act in ways that are faithful? Explain.
- What are some examples of how people might claim to be faithful but their actions are not consistent with such a faith?
- Why is it important to act with love, as our faith teaches?
- How would our Church and world be different if those who attend Scripture studies, Sunday Mass, or religious education classes were to *never* act on what they heard?
- How do our actions reveal what is truly in our hearts?
- How can doing charitable and virtuous works help increase our faith?

Taking My Scripture Home

Who is someone you truly admire for his or her faith and actions? How can you tell that person has a strong faith? What do your actions and priorities reveal about the things you believe?

MARK 8:27–35

This passage begins with Peter brilliantly identifying Jesus as the Christ. This was an important revelation that Jesus did not want shared at the time. But soon, Jesus rebukes St. Peter for completely missing the point about the necessity of the suffering and death Jesus had to endure. So important is the cross that Jesus makes it an essential part of the lives of those who wish to follow him.

- Why do you suppose people thought Jesus was a prophet or John the Baptist?
- How do you think Peter was able to identify Jesus as the Christ?
- How does studying the Scriptures and praying help us recognize God's presence in our lives?
- Why did Peter rebuke Jesus about all that talk of suffering, dying, and rising from the dead?
- Jesus was stern with Peter and accused him of not thinking like God. What are some ways people today attempt to limit God's love, forgiveness, or power?
- What do you suppose Jesus meant by saying whoever loses his life for the gospel's sake will save it, but those who try to save their life will lose it?

- What are some examples of how people today dedicate their lives to serving others and God?
- Which do you believe will bring you more joy in life, serving your own interests or giving your life to the service of God and others? Explain.

Taking My Scripture Home

When in your life have you acted with total love and concern for another person without any regard for your own interests? How did you feel when the other person realized your good will toward him or her? How would the world be different if everyone could experience how you felt then?

Twenty-fifth Sunday of Ordinary Time

WISDOM 2:12, 17–20

This passage from Wisdom speaks of the perspective of the wicked. Some experts believe this passage is a prediction of Jesus' death.

- Why would someone who is good be obnoxious to someone who is wicked?
- Have you seen this situation in today's society?
- What is the risk of being godly in today's world?
- How are the good in today's world tested by society?
- Do you believe those who love God will be protected by God? Explain.
- How is this passage similar to what Jesus experienced in his life and death?

Taking My Scripture Home

How are you tested in your everyday life? How can Jesus' example of dependence on God help you when you are tested?

RESPONSORIAL PSALM REFLECTION: PSALM 54:6b

- How does God uphold life?
- What does this verse tell us about the Psalmist's dependence on God?

JAMES 3:16—4:3

In this passage the author continues his discourse on morality. The author contrasts the wisdom of above in the first part of this passage to the wisdom of Earth in the second part.

- What are some of the adjectives the author uses for wisdom from above?
- Describe the type of person who has these characteristics.
- Why is it obvious that the person described in James would have heavenly wisdom?
- Who in your life would you describe as having heavenly wisdom?
- The author describes heavenly wisdom as *pure*. What do you suppose this means?
- How is heavenly wisdom contrasted with the behavior described in the second part of the reading?
- How can the descriptions in the second part of this reading be applied to today's society?

Taking My Scripture Home

What can you do each day to increase your heavenly wisdom? How can you keep your thoughts and motives free from earthly wisdom?

MARK 9:30–37

This passage provides insights about the difficulty the disciples had understanding Jesus. While traveling through Galilee, Jesus explained the importance of his suffering, death, and resurrection. The disciples did not understand, but they were afraid to question him and too preoccupied with the question of who among them was the greatest.

- Why do you suppose Jesus did not want the crowds to know about his journey through Galilee?
- Jesus earlier told the disciples he would suffer and die. Why do you think he brought the subject up again?
- Why do you think the disciples were afraid to ask questions?
- Why might the disciples have been afraid to tell Jesus about their argument?
- What did Jesus teach the disciples about being the greatest?
- How is that teaching different from the viewpoint of society today?
- What does it mean to be a *servant?*
- Why do you think Jesus used a child as an illustration?
- Who in today's society are powerless and defenseless?
- What does it mean to receive someone in Jesus' name?

Taking My Scripture Home

What are some ways you can be a servant? This week, how can you serve someone who has no power or status? Who can you receive in Jesus' name?

Twenty-sixth Sunday of Ordinary Time

NUMBERS 11:25–29

The book of Numbers continues the Exodus story of the Israelites' journey into the Promised Land. The seventy elders mentioned in this passage would assist Moses in leading the Israelites.

- Moses chose seventy elders to help him lead the people. How do you think Moses made his choices?
- What qualities do people look for in their leaders?
- How are Christians called to be leaders?
- This passage describes God taking some of Moses' spirit and passing it to the elders. How do people share their spirit with others today?
- What happens to a school, parish, or company when people are enthusiastic about it?
- A young man became jealous that Eldad and Medad were prophesying. Why do you suppose Moses said that he wished all people might receive God's Spirit?

Taking My Scripture Home

What leadership qualities do you possess? How can you use those qualities this week to lead someone closer to God? How can you use your enthusiasm to promote God's love to others?

RESPONSORIAL PSALM REFLECTION: PSALM 19:9a

- What is a *precept*?
- How can instruction bring us joy?
- How can chaotic lives cause distress?

JAMES 5:1—6

In this era it was widely believed that wealth was a sign of God's approval while poverty was a sign of God's punishment for sins. Many laborers were not given a just wage. This passage has much in common with the Beatitudes.

- Why do you think the author of this passage reminded the rich that their wealth would someday be worthless?
- The author warns the wealthy of future suffering. How do you think the wealthy suffered?
- What are some examples of how people today trust in their wealth?
- In what or whom do Christians trust?
- In the reading what do the laborers do?
- How do people mistreat others today?
- Why would the laborers be considered righteous in this passage?

Taking My Scripture Home

In what ways do you trust wealth above God? How can the poor be an inspiration to trust in God instead of material wealth?

MARK 9:38—43, 45, 47—48

In this passage Jesus is again teaching his disciples. This time Jesus addresses them in a house in Capernaum. Jesus' words echo those of Moses in the first reading.

- Why was John upset in this passage?
- What did Jesus say?
- Where in today's society do you see groups who believe their perspective is the only right one?
- What do you think Jesus would say to such groups?
- Jesus goes on to speak of those who offer a cup water to others. Who are people you know that help others?
- What and where is *Gehenna?*
- Jesus speaks about sacrificing those things that keep us apart from God or cause us to sin. In today's society what are some things that people hold onto that keep them apart from God?

Taking My Scripture Home

What in your life causes you to sin? How can sacrificing those things bring you closer to God?

Twenty-seventh Sunday of Ordinary Time

GENESIS 2:18–24

This story from Genesis is designed to show that marital union between man and woman is a good and natural part of God's design. The life that comes from this union is also blessed and good in God's eyes.

- What do you suppose the author meant by saying that it is not good for people to be alone?
- What are some blessings that come to people who fall in love and marry?
- How does a marriage based in God's love bring peace and joy to the couple's children?
- How do good marriages benefit the community?
- In this story God creates a woman from the rib of a man. What do you suppose this symbolism might say about God's plan for marriage?
- What are some ways people can build good marriages?

Taking My Scripture Home

What are some ways you can reach out to those who may be lonely or in need of a friend? What can you do to deepen your respect for life in all its forms?

RESPONSORIAL PSALM REFLECTION: PSALM 128:5

- How does the Lord bless us?
- How do you feel knowing that you depend on God's blessings?

HEBREWS 2:9–11

In this passage the author is referencing Psalm 8 in an attempt to explain how Jesus was humbled, suffered greatly, and returned to his glory above all others.

- What do you suppose the author meant by saying Jesus was made lower than angels for a while?
- Why would suffering make Jesus perfect?
- How can our own suffering make us more empathetic to the struggles of others?
- How could you use this passage to describe the humility of Jesus?
- How would the world be different if those who held positions of power were as humble as Jesus?
- What do you suppose it means to be considered a brother or sister of Jesus?

Taking My Scripture Home

What are some ways you can imitate the humility of Jesus? What can you do this week to reach out to someone who is struggling or suffering?

MARK 10:2–16

This Gospel brings together the first reading's theme of respect for marriage and the second reading's theme of humility. Regarding marriage, Jesus makes it clear that permanent marriages reflect God's plan. In the second part Jesus uses the children as an example of the utter dependence we must have on God in order to enter the kingdom.

- Why do you suppose the Pharisees were trying to test Jesus?
- Instead of quoting the law of Moses, Jesus went beyond the law and spoke of God's plan for marriage. Why did Jesus do this?
- Why is it important to understand the intent or spirit of a law?
- Why do you suppose the Church grants annulments today?
- In the second part of this reading how did Jesus feel when the disciples reprimanded the people for bringing their children to him?
- What did Jesus mean when he said the kingdom of God belongs to those who are childlike?
- Did the disciples act in a way that showed they understood this teaching of Jesus? Explain.
- Who are some people you know who are trusting and dependent on God?

Taking My Scripture Home

What can you do to become more dependent on God? Why is it important to deepen your dependence on God? What must you let go of in order to become more trusting of God?

Twenty-eighth Sunday of Ordinary Time

WISDOM 7:7–11

This passage is part of an entire section of the book of Wisdom that speaks of the significance of wisdom and the brilliance of those who are wise. In this passage Solomon describes how he acquired wisdom. Like the Proverbs reading on the Twentieth Sunday of Ordinary Time, wisdom is given a feminine pronoun.

- The author writes that prudence and wisdom were given to Solomon. What does the word *prudence* mean?
- What is the difference between wisdom and being book-smart?
- What did Solomon do to receive prudence and wisdom?
- Why is prayer important?
- Give some examples of situations today in which the best action to take would be to pray for wisdom before proceeding.
- In this passage Solomon values wisdom above all other assets. How would today's world be different if everyone had the same philosophy?

Taking My Scripture Home

How much do you value wisdom? How often do you pray for wisdom? How would your world be different if you valued wisdom above everything else in your life?

RESPONSORIAL PSALM REFLECTION: PSALM 90:14

- How are love and joy interrelated?
- How can being joyful lead to love for others?

HEBREWS 4:12–13

Experts believe the book of Hebrews was often attached to letters sent to Christian communities. It served as a model for Christian living and encouraged early Christians in their struggles.

- The author describes God's Word as living and active. What do you suppose this means?
- Why is it important today for God's Word to be living and active?
- In what ways have you seen God's Word alive in others?
- What does it mean for something to be a *two-edged sword?*
- What are some examples of situations today that are two-edged swords, or difficult regardless of the choices made?
- How is following God sometimes difficult?
- How is living apart from God difficult?
- How do you feel knowing that nothing is concealed from God?

Taking My Scripture Home

How is God's Word living and active in your life? What choices can you make each day to keep God's Word alive and active?

MARK 10:17–30

In Jesus' time being rich was considered to be a blessing from God. Those who were wealthy and enjoyed good fortune were in God's favor. Those who were poor or sick had done something to provoke God or make God angry. Therefore, the message of Jesus to give away wealth was radical and challenged the people's image of God.

- In this Gospel Jesus challenges the man to do more than just follow the commandments. What was the challenge?
- Why would this be a challenge for the man?
- In Jesus' time wealth was considered a favor from God. Do you think that is still the belief today? Explain.
- How does society view wealth and material possessions?
- How can wealth and material possessions make people feel secure or accepted by others?
- This man went away, unsure he could meet Jesus' challenge. How does Jesus' message challenge us today?
- What do you think happened to this confused man?
- What changes must happen to a person before he or she begins to look for happiness not in material possessions, but in following Jesus' teachings?
- Jesus implies that following the commandments is just the beginning of leading a Christian life. What are some examples of ways Christians go beyond the Ten Commandments with their actions and attitudes?

- Who do you know in your own life whose actions and attitudes show he or she is a Christian?

Taking My Scripture Home

What specific ways do you depend on material possessions for security and acceptance? How does the challenge of the man in the Gospel apply to your life? What actions or attitudes can you change in your own life to meet this challenge?

Twenty-ninth Sunday of Ordinary Time

ISAIAH 53:10–11

This passage is taken from the last of the four Servant Songs found in the book of Isaiah. Obviously Jesus perfectly fits the description of the one who must suffer as atonement for the sins of all.

- What did the author intend to convey by saying that *the Lord was pleased to crush him?*
- Who do you suppose might be considered the descendants of the Suffering Servant?
- What was the will of the Lord that was accomplished through Jesus?
- This passage was written hundreds of years before Christ's birth. What sort of expectations and anticipation do you suppose these words created in the hearts of those who read this?
- What does it mean to bear their guilt?
- What does this say about a God who sends such a perfect Suffering Servant to save humanity?

Taking My Scripture Home

How do you feel knowing Jesus suffered and sacrificed his life so that people today might know God more intimately? How can your actions and attitudes reveal your gratitude for Jesus' sacrifice?

RESPONSORIAL PSALM REFLECTION: PSALM 33:22

- How can we place our trust in God?
- What keeps us from placing our trust in God?
- How does God's mercy and forgiveness make it easy to trust the Lord?

HEBREWS 4:14–16

The author refers to Jesus as the great high priest, thereby establishing him as greater than the Jewish high priests. This passage introduces the theme of Jesus as high priest in the letter to the Hebrews.

- What images come to mind when you think of Jesus as the great high priest?
- Why do you suppose Jesus is able to sympathize with the weaknesses of people?
- Jesus was tempted every way, yet he never sinned. How do you suppose this temptation helped Jesus understand humanity?
- The author speaks of confidently approaching Jesus, that we might find grace and help. Why is it important to approach God with confidence?
- Why do we need to receive mercy?
- What is God's grace?
- How does God's grace help people?
- Who do you know that seems to be filled with God's grace?

Taking My Scripture Home

How can you pray with more confidence and trust? What are some reasons for having confidence in God's love?

MARK 10:35–45

In Jesus' day it was common to refer to one's destiny as the cup God gives a person to drink. James and John certainly did not understand the suffering and death Jesus was to endure or that they, too, were called to share in that destiny.

- Why do you suppose James and John wanted to sit at Jesus' right and left?
- What are some examples of how people today want power and glory at the expense of others?
- How did Jesus respond to James and John's request?
- How do you suppose the other ten disciples felt when they figured out what James and John were up to?
- What effect do greed and selfishness have on a community?
- What did Jesus say was the key to being great in the kingdom?
- What does it mean to be a servant?
- What are some examples of the type of service Jesus is speaking about?

Taking My Scripture Home

Jesus speaks about a spirit of service. Who are some people in your life that seem to have this spirit? What can you do this week to truly serve the needs of others?

Thirtieth Sunday of Ordinary Time

JEREMIAH 31:7–9

This passage was taken from the early preaching of Jeremiah. Originally it was believed that he was speaking of the return of the ten lost tribes from the former northern part of Israel that had been in exile in Assyria. When they never returned, other interpretations were given to this oracle. In this passage the Ephraim mentioned is the name of a tribe.

- How do you suppose the people who read this passage felt about the image of the Israelites returning home?
- How would you feel if you were allowed to return home after spending a long time away unwillingly?
- How does God's love bring people together today?
- What image of God comes to mind when you read this passage?
- What qualities of a loving father can be attributed to God?

Taking My Scripture Home

When have you felt alone or alienated from others? How can you reach out to others who may be feeling this way?

RESPONSORIAL PSALM REFLECTION: PSALM 126:3

- What are some great things the Lord has done?
- Why does God's greatness fill people with joy?
- What does it mean to be filled with joy?

HEBREWS 5:1–6

The author draws an analogy between the high priests of the Old Testament and Christ to illustrate how God glorified Jesus. Because Jesus was fully human, he was able to be the perfect high priest for humanity. Melchizedek was the greatest high priest of the Old Testament. Aaron was the brother of Moses and helped lead the Israelites out of Egyptian captivity. The second quote in this passage is from Psalm 110:4.

- What was the role of the high priests?
- What were some of the things high priests did according to this passage?
- The author speaks of how Aaron was called by God. How do you suppose people today can tell if they are being called to clerical, religious life, or other vocations?
- What are some similarities between the role and qualities of the high priest and the role and qualities of Jesus?
- The author makes the point that God glorified Jesus. What do you suppose this means?
- Jesus was fully human although he was the Son of God. How do you suppose Jesus' humanity helped God relate to the condition of all people?
- What can you tell about a God who goes to such lengths to reach out to people?

Taking My Scripture Home

What are some shortcomings and weaknesses in your life? How can these imperfections help you become more patient and tolerant of others?

MARK 10:46–52

This story also appears twice in Matthew's Gospel. Since Mark placed this story just before Jesus' entry into Jerusalem, some believe the healing of the blind man may be symbolic of how the disciples' eyes would be opened once they witnessed the death and resurrection of Jesus in the days ahead.

- What can you tell about Bartimaeus from this story?
- How did Bartimaeus show his faith in Jesus?
- What are some ways people today show their faith in God?
- What struggles did Bartimaeus face in getting an audience with Jesus?
- What struggles might people your age face trying to live their Christian values?
- Bartimaeus was not shy about telling Jesus what he wanted. Why is it good for us to place our needs and desires before God in prayer?
- Why do you suppose Jesus told Bartimaeus that his faith had saved him?
- How can faith heal divisions and hard feelings among people today?

- What did Bartimaeus do after he was healed?
- What can people do today to follow Jesus?

Taking My Scripture Home

What are some dreams, hopes, or needs you would like to bring before God? How can you see more clearly the divine spark inside the people you meet every day?

Thirty-first Sunday of Ordinary Time

DEUTERONOMY 6:2—6

Deuteronomy means "second law," but it truly is a reiteration and commentary on the law that was given to Moses on Mount Sinai. In this passage the author summarizes the entire theme of Deuteronomy by quoting the most important part of the law.

- What does it mean to *fear the Lord?*
- According to the author what benefit awaited those who kept the Lord's commandments?
- What benefit comes to people today who respect the Lord and enjoy a close relationship with God?
- Is it really possible to command someone to love God? Explain.
- What attitudes, reflections, or actions might help a person begin to love God?
- How can you tell if a person is in love with someone?
- How can you tell if someone truly loves God?

Taking My Scripture Home

What can you do to fall in love with God? What are some ways you can express your love for God?

RESPONSORIAL PSALM REFLECTION: PSALM 18:2

- What does it mean to love the Lord?
- Why do you love the Lord?
- How does God give you strength?

HEBREWS 7:23–28

In the book of Genesis a brief passage (14:17–20) describes Melchizedek, a priest of God, meeting Abram and blessing him after his victory in war. Since nothing is written about Melchizedek's past or future, Melchizedek became a figure for an unending priesthood. This passage is taken from the author's attempt to describe Jesus as the never-ending priest.

- Why is it comforting to know Jesus lives forever?
- What is the role of a priest?
- How does Jesus fulfill the role of the perfect priest?
- How is Jesus able to save people who approach God through him?
- The priests of the Old Testament offered sacrifices to atone for their sins and for the sins of the people. What sacrifice did Jesus offer for people?
- How did Jesus' sacrifice atone for the sins of all people?
- How would you explain the motive of an innocent person who would willingly take the blame and punishment for something that another person did?
- How must God have felt toward humanity to offer Jesus as the perfect sacrifice?

Taking My Scripture Home

How do you feel knowing God has forgiven your weaknesses? How can you show mercy and forgiveness to others this week?

MARK 12:28b–34

This passage takes up the theme introduced in the first reading. In the time of Jesus many leaders pondered which was the greatest commandment. Here, Jesus links the love of God with the love of others. The sacrifice Jesus made for the sins of all makes burnt offerings and sacrifices unnecessary.

- Why do you suppose love of God is the greatest commandment?
- What does it mean to love God with *all your heart, soul, and mind?*
- If we are to love our neighbor as ourselves, how would you describe the sort of self-love Jesus was referring to?
- Why do you suppose Jesus emphasized the love of others and ourselves as the second greatest commandment?
- What does true love for others entail?
- Describe someone in your life who seems to love God and others.
- Why do you suppose Jesus told the scribe that he was not far from God's kingdom?
- Why do you suppose no one dared ask Jesus any more questions after this conversation?

Taking My Scripture Home

What can you do to open your heart to God's love? How can you trust God's love to guide you through your life?

Thirty-second Sunday of Ordinary Time

1 KINGS 17:10–16

Elijah is considered the greatest of the Old Testament prophets. In this passage the Lord had sent a drought over the land because the Israelites had worshiped Baal. The Lord arranged for a widow to provide for Elijah during this time.

- How would you describe the widow's financial situation?
- What else can you tell about the widow from her actions toward Elijah?
- How did the Lord provide for the widow, her son, and Elijah?
- What are some ways the Lord provides for people today?
- When is it difficult to trust God to provide for us?
- The widow trusted the Lord and shared her food with Elijah even though she had very little. How can our generosity to others make a difference in today's world?

Taking My Scripture Home

How has the Lord provided for you and your family? What can you do to share your blessings with others?

RESPONSORIAL PSALM REFLECTION: PSALM 146:1b

- Why is the Lord worthy of your praise?
- What are some ways we praise the Lord with our actions?
- How can our attitudes and speech praise God?

HEBREWS 9:24–28

In Old Testament times animals were slaughtered and sacrificed annually as atonement for sins. The author in this passage is making the case that Christ sacrificed his own blood, which was infinitely more valuable than any sacrifice made before. So perfect was this sacrifice that it needed to be done only once for all time.

- What sacrifices are being compared in this passage?
- What is different about the animal sacrifices made in Old Testament times and the sacrifice Jesus made?
- Why do you suppose Jesus only had to make one sacrifice in order to take away sin for all time?
- Why will Jesus come a second time according to this passage?
- What does it mean to say our sins are forgiven because of Jesus?
- Why is it important to understand the good news of our forgiveness?
- What difference do you suppose this understanding of forgiveness made to those who had always sacrificed animals as atonement for sins?

Taking My Scripture Home

Do you truly believe God loves you exactly as you are and will forgive all of your sins? How can you extend forgiveness and mercy to others?

MARK 12:38–44

This passage is also found in Luke's Gospel. The contrast between the false piety and pretense of the Pharisees and the real generosity of the widow makes a stunning image in this passage.

- Why did Jesus warn about the behavior of the scribes?
- What was it about their behavior that Jesus found objectionable?
- Why do you suppose Jesus said these scribes would receive a severe condemnation?
- How do you think the scribes felt when they heard what Jesus said?
- Why did Jesus say the widow who contributed two cents gave more than the rich who put in great sums?
- Why do you think the poor widow impressed Jesus so much?
- What are some ways people today can show their gratitude and trust in God?
- How can people make their entire life a contribution to God?
- Why do some people find it difficult to be generous?
- Besides money, what can people your age give to others?

Taking My Scripture Home

Who do you know that may be in need of friendship, forgiveness, or someone to talk with? What can you do to extend generosity to that person?

Thirty-third Sunday of Ordinary Time

DANIEL 12:1–3

Daniel's description of a resurrection provided significant hope for the Jewish people who suffered persecution at the time. Jewish people believed that the reward for a just life was to live to see one's great-grandchildren. When Jews began to be put to death for following the law, some lost heart. This vision of a resurrection provided a new perspective and new hope for those who were faithful to God.

- The author writes of a time of great distress and how a leader will save the people. How do you suppose the Jews who were being persecuted felt when hearing these words?
- What are some situations today where people need support, encouragement, and hope to help them persevere?
- The idea of resurrection is nothing new to Christians. However, at the time of Daniel, people did not openly embrace this idea. How do you suppose the Jewish people felt about the idea of resurrection?
- What do you suppose was the difference between those who were to be a disgrace upon resurrection and those who were to live forever?
- Who are the wise people that are to shine brightly?
- How do people lead others to justice?
- Who are some people today that lead us to justice?

Taking My Scripture Home

What can you do to be an inspiration to others? How does Christ's resurrection provide hope and encouragement to you?

RESPONSORIAL PSALM REFLECTION: PSALM 16:1

- What does it mean to inherit the Lord?
- Who is it that allowed you to inherit the Lord?
- How can you pass God's love on to others?

HEBREWS 10:11–14, 18

An important role of the Jewish priests was to offer daily sacrifices for atonement of their sins and the sins of the people. These actions were not considered a removal of sin, but a way of showing repentance. By contrast, the author points out that Jesus' sacrifice is complete and perfect, removing the need for daily sacrifice.

- What is the sacrifice Jesus offered for sins?
- Why do you suppose this sacrifice brings forgiveness and mercy to all?
- This change in the need for daily sacrifice was a significantly new way to think about God for the Jewish people. If God required daily sacrifices, how do you suppose the Jewish people imagined their relationship with God?
- What did the need for daily sacrifices say about their sins and God's feelings toward those sins?
- If God no longer required daily ritual sacrifice because of the sacrifice of Jesus, what do you suppose changed about the way the people saw their relationship with God?
- How do you suppose the people felt knowing they were forgiven?

Taking My Scripture Home

How do you feel knowing God has forgiven you of all your sins? What can you do to share this mercy at times when others have hurt you?

MARK 13:24–32

This passage is a discourse by Jesus about his return to Earth. Similar to Daniel's attempt in the first reading to comfort a persecuted people, Jesus is trying to provide hope to those who face suffering and oppression.

- Are passages about the end of time cause for alarm? Explain.
- What are some ways people have a tendency to read too much into predictions about the last days?
- What do you suppose was the purpose Jesus had in mind for speaking of this end time?
- Why do you suppose Jesus says that only the Father knows the time when the final hour will occur?
- What can people do to prepare for their own final hour?

- How do you suppose people might act if they knew for sure that Jesus was to return tomorrow?
- What comfort does it bring to know that, no matter how or when the world ends, the faithful are promised everlasting life?

Taking My Scripture Home

In what areas of your life do you feel you need more conversion to God? How can you open your heart to God and trust more deeply in these areas?

Thirty-fourth Sunday of Ordinary Time

This Sunday is also the celebration of the solemnity of Christ the King.

DANIEL 7:13—14

This passage from Daniel is an appropriate choice, as it speaks of a vision that is highly reminiscent of Jesus. In fact Jesus borrowed the term "Son of man" as a reference to himself.

- Daniel's vision speaks of a Son of man coming on clouds and reaching the Ancient One. Who do you suppose the Son of man represents?
- Who is the Ancient One?
- Why do you suppose the Son of man received glory and kingship?
- Why is it good to think of Jesus as king?
- How do people act around a king?
- Why is Jesus worthy of our worship and praise?

Taking My Scripture Home

How can you let Jesus be the king of your heart? How can you become more of a loyal servant to God?

RESPONSORIAL PSALM REFLECTION: PSALM 93:1a

- What does it mean to be *robed with majesty?*
- How do you let the Lord rule your life?
- How do you praise the Lord?

REVELATION 1:5–8

The book of Revelation has many things in common with the book of Daniel. The author uses symbolism extensively to create an image of hope for an oppressed people. This passage echoes the passage from Daniel in the first reading, with wonderful visions of Jesus coming to rule at the end times.

- What does it mean to be *the firstborn of the dead?*
- How did Jesus free us from our sins?
- How did Jesus make us a kingdom?
- What are some ways Jesus showed his love for humanity?
- What does it mean to be *the Alpha and the Omega?*
- How is Jesus present in the world right now?
- How would the world be different if everyone were to allow Jesus to rule his or her heart?

Taking My Scripture Home

What can you do to help build the kingdom of God? How can this passage comfort you in times of struggle?

JOHN 18:33b–37

This passage is taken from the Passion account while Jesus is on trial before Pontius Pilate. Once again the theme of Jesus as king marks this week's celebration. Interestingly, Jesus refers to a kingdom not of this world over which he rules.

- Why do you suppose Pilate asked Jesus if he were the king of the Jews?
- Why did the Jews hand Jesus over to Pilate?
- What are some ways people today are fearful of Jesus' message?
- How would you describe the kingdom of God?
- What does it mean to testify to the truth?
- What do you suppose is the truth Jesus came to testify about?
- What does it mean to belong to the truth?
- How do people's actions and attitudes show that they listen to the truth?
- How can people today listen to Jesus' voice?

Taking My Scripture Home

How can your actions and values show others that you belong to God's kingdom? How can you welcome others into God's kingdom?

The Solemnity of the Most Holy Trinity

DEUTERONOMY 4:32–34, 39–40

This passage is part of a speech Moses makes to the Israelites before they enter the Promised Land. By inviting the Israelites to reflect on the great things God has done for them, Moses emphasizes the nearness of God to God's people.

- Why do you think Moses asked questions to make a point?
- What were some of the points that Moses was trying to make?
- Moses speaks of the great things that God had done for the Israelites. What were some of the great things God had done?
- How did these things prove to the Israelites that their God was the only God?
- What are some great things that God does for us today?
- Why did Moses stress the importance of the statutes and commandments?
- In what ways can people prosper when living a faithful life?

Taking My Scripture Home

How can you remember all the great things God has done for you? How can remembering these blessings help you live a more faithful life?

RESPONSORIAL PSALM REFLECTION: PSALM 33:12b

- What does it mean to be chosen by God?
- As Catholics we believe that we, too, are a chosen people. What are the responsibilities of God's chosen people?
- What blessings come with being chosen?

ROMANS 8:14—17

The letter to the Romans was written before St. Paul visited Rome around AD 56. In this section of Romans, St. Paul teaches us that the Spirit of God dwells within us, enabling us to call God our Father. The Trinity is not just outside us.

- What is the difference between a slave and a son or daughter?
- How would a slave address a master?
- Why would a slave be fearful of a master?
- How would a child address a loving father?
- How would a child feel in the presence of a loving father?
- Why would being an heir of God cause us to suffer in this life?
- How can things such as peer pressure and society's values make it difficult to follow God today?
- What are some consequences for not following society's values?
- What is the reward for following God?

Taking My Scripture Home

How can imagining God as a loving parent help you grow closer to God? Why does becoming closer to God make it easier to stand against peer pressure and society's values? What actions can you do each day that will bring you closer to God?

MATTHEW 28:16—20

After the resurrection in Matthew's Gospel, an angel tells Mary Magdalene and the other Mary to send the disciples to meet Jesus in Galilee. This passage is the account of that meeting in Galilee—the last words Jesus speaks to his disciples. These concluding verses of Matthew's Gospel, the Great Commission, proclaim the Trinitarian formula we use in baptism and the Christian life.

- Why do you suppose the disciples doubted Jesus when they saw him?
- What were some of the horrific events that had recently happened to Jesus?
- How do you think the disciples felt when they saw Jesus alive?
- What did Jesus tell the disciples to do?
- Why was it important for the disciples to baptize and teach?
- How does the Church still follow these instructions today?
- Why would it have been comforting for the disciples to hear that Jesus was with them always?
- How can this message comfort us today?

Taking My Scripture Home

How can your attitudes, words, and actions teach others about God's love? How does the assurance that Jesus is always with you bring peace to you no matter what happens in your life?

The Solemnity of the Most Holy Body and Blood of Christ

EXODUS 24:3–8

The sprinkling of animal blood was a ceremonial rite or ritual that sealed a covenant or promise between two parties. Animals were also slaughtered and sacrificed as an offering for sins. This passage occurs after God gives the Israelites the Ten Commandments and other laws. The Jewish people accepted the laws, became God's people, and celebrated this covenant by sacrificing animals.

- In this passage the Lord spoke to Moses. Why do you think God chose Moses?
- The Jewish people agreed to all the laws and ordinances of God. What are some laws of God that we follow today?
- The Jewish people answered Moses with one voice. What does that tell you about the commitment and dedication of the people?
- What are some examples of how large groups of people speak with one voice today?
- Moses built an altar and twelve pillars at the foot of the mountain. Why do you think he built twelve?
- Twelve is often used throughout the Bible to symbolize God's people; it's also used as a perfect, or complete number. What are some other things or people that are grouped in twelve in the Bible?
- Why do you think the blood of animals was significant to the Jewish people?
- How are blood and covenants significant for Catholics today?

Taking My Scripture Home

What law of God is the most difficult for you to follow? How can remembering the covenant at Mass help you follow God's law of love?

RESPONSORIAL PSALM REFLECTION: PSALM 116:13

- This Psalm response contains two action verbs. What are they?
- How can someone actually take the cup of salvation?
- Why would someone call on the name of God?

HEBREWS 9:11–15

Animals were sacrificed annually for the atonement of sins. The author in this passage is making the case that Christ's sacrifice is much more valuable than any sacrifice of animals. Because of the sacrifice of Christ's own blood, we are freed from sin and able to inherit a life with God.

- Why would Jesus' sacrifice be more perfect than the sacrifice of animals?
- Why do we believe our sins are forgiven because of Jesus?
- Why is it important to understand and believe the good news of our forgiveness?
- How can Jesus' death bring us into a covenant with God?
- The author speaks of *dead works* in this passage. What do you suppose the author means by this?
- How do we worship a *living God?*

Taking My Scripture Home

How can you believe more fully that God has forgiven you of all your sins? How can you extend that forgiveness and mercy to others?

MARK 14:12–16, 22–26

This passage is also part of the Gospel reading from Passion/Palm Sunday. The feast of Unleavened Bread is also called the Passover Feast. This feast commemorates the Jewish people being freed from Egyptian slavery. This passage particularly emphasizes the necessity of preparing well for the celebration, something we should do before every Eucharist.

- How do you think the disciples felt finding everything in the city as Jesus had described?
- How could knowing minor details were arranged help bring a feeling of security and peace to the disciples?
- How do you think Jesus felt knowing this was the last meal he would eat with his friends?
- Jesus named the bread and wine as his body and blood. Why do you think this was important?
- What significance did this action have for the disciples gathered there?

- What is the significance for us today?
- Why do you suppose the words of Jesus are repeated during the Eucharistic Prayer?

Taking My Scripture Home

How can you become more attentive to the words of the Eucharistic Prayer? How can these words bring you into a closer relationship with God?

The Nativity of St. John the Baptist

June 24

ISAIAH 49:1–6

This passage is the second of the four "Servant Songs" in the book of Isaiah. The Servant Songs describe the ideal leader as one who serves. This passage is also read at Mass on Tuesday of Holy Week.

- This passage speaks of how God called the servant from birth and named the servant. Does everyone or just a few chosen people have a calling from God? Explain.
- Who do you know in your own life that seems to have a calling from God?
- The servant is described as a *sharp-edged sword* and a *polished arrow*. What type of person does this bring to mind?
- The servant seems to think he or she has failed with his or her mission on Earth. Why do you suppose the servant would feel this way?
- How can knowing the feelings of this servant help us at times when we fail to spread God's love to others?
- In this passage does the servant depend on his own strength or God? Explain.
- What is God's mission for this servant?

Taking My Scripture Home

The servant is described as a *sharp-edged sword* and a *polished arrow*. How do you challenge society's values? In what ways are you a servant leader?

RESPONSORIAL PSALM REFLECTION: PSALM 139:14a

- Do you believe you are wonderfully made? Explain.
- Do you believe everyone is wonderfully made? Explain.
- How would the world be different if everyone had the utmost respect for life?

ACTS 13:22–26

This passage is part of an address that St. Paul gave to the Jewish community at the synagogue in Antioch. St. Paul recounts the history of salvation and the progression of Christianity through Jesus. He notes the role of John the Baptist.

- Why was it important that St. Paul remind the Jewish community of their history?
- Who was David and why was David a significant king?
- John the Baptist urged the people of Israel to repent. What does it mean to repent?
- Do you feel repentance is important in our daily lives? Explain.
- John the Baptist had an important role in preparing the people of Israel for the coming of Jesus. In what ways are Christians called to do the same?
- How did John the Baptist compare himself to Jesus?
- Why is being humble important?

Taking My Scripture Home

Where do you need repentance in your own life? How can you humbly accept the mission of proclaiming God's love to everyone?

LUKE 1:57–66, 80

The Gospel of Luke is the only Gospel to record the story of the birth of John the Baptist. Both Zechariah and Elizabeth were elderly and had no children. The angel Gabriel appeared to Zechariah to tell him Elizabeth would have a son and they would name him John. Zechariah questioned the angel. Because of his disbelief in the angel, Zechariah was unable to speak until John the Baptist was born.

- Why do you suppose it was so important for women to have children in those days?
- How do you think Elizabeth and Zechariah felt during those years when they were unable to have children?
- After John was born, Zechariah could speak again and he blessed God. What does that say about Zechariah?
- Why was this birth a miracle to Zechariah?
- The neighbors discussed events surrounding this birth. What do you think the neighbors talked about?
- What does it mean to be *strong in spirit?*
- What habits do you suppose John the Baptist practiced each day to become strong in spirit?

Taking My Scripture Home

How often do you thank God for all the miracles in your life? What habits can you practice each day to become even stronger in spirit?

The Transfiguration of the Lord

August 6

DANIEL 7:9–10, 13–14

The book of Daniel is similar to the book of Revelation in that it uses symbolism and symbolic language to convey hope to people during a time of persecution. This passage from Daniel speaks of a vision that is highly reminiscent of Jesus. Jesus borrowed the term "Son of man" to refer to himself.

- This passage gives a description of the *Ancient One*. Who do you think the *Ancient One* represents?
- Daniel's vision speaks of a *Son of man* coming on clouds and reaching the *Ancient One*. Who do you suppose the *Son of man* represents?
- Why do you suppose the *Son of man* received glory and kingship?
- Why is it good to think of Jesus as king?
- How do people act around a king?
- Why is Jesus worthy of our worship and praise?

Taking My Scripture Home

How can you let Jesus be king of your heart? How can you become a more loyal servant to God?

RESPONSORIAL PSALM REFLECTION: PSALM 97:1a, 9a

- What does it mean to say the Lord is the most high?
- Why should we reflect on the kingship of God?
- What are some characteristics of someone who believes in the kingship of God?

2 PETER 1:16–19

The second letter of Peter was written to remind readers of Jesus and his teachings. It was also an encouragement to those who were beginning to doubt whether Jesus would come again. The "we" in this passage refers to Peter, James, and John, the disciples who were with Jesus at the transfiguration.

- Why would it be important to listen to someone who was an eyewitness of such an event?
- What had Peter, James, and John witnessed?
- Why would the transfiguration bring Jesus honor and glory?
- Why do you suppose Peter, James, and John were present during the transfiguration?
- What effect do you suppose hearing the voice of God had on Peter, James, and John?
- The author draws an analogy between paying attention to this message and a lamp in the dark. What symbolism could be associated with this analogy?

Taking My Scripture Home

Do you listen for the voice of God in your own life? What can you do to pay more attention to God's presence every moment of your day?

MARK 9:2–10

The transfiguration of Jesus was a sign to help the disciples understand that Jesus shared in the glory of God. Moses represented the law and Elijah represented the prophets. Their presence on Mount Sinai with Jesus symbolically showed that Jesus was about to fulfill the law and prophecy with his death and resurrection.

- The significance of Jesus' death and resurrection must have been difficult for the disciples to appreciate before his death. How do you think this sign helped the disciples understand who Jesus was?
- Do you suppose this episode had more meaning for the disciples after Jesus rose from the dead? Explain.
- Today some people do not have proper reverence or appreciation for the significance of God's presence in their lives. Why do you suppose some people struggle to appreciate God's presence?
- What are some miracles that we see every day that show us God's glory?
- What are some ways we can deepen our appreciation and reverence for God?
- In this passage the voice instructed the disciples to listen to Jesus, *the beloved Son*. Where do we hear God's voice in our lives?
- How can listening to and taking to heart Jesus' message transfigure our attitudes and lives?

Taking My Scripture Home

How can your actions and attitudes reveal that you listen to God's Word in your life? How can you look for God's presence in all the experiences of your life?

The Assumption of the Blessed Virgin Mary

August 15
Mass During the Day

REVELATION 11:19a; 12:1—6a, 10ab

The book of Revelation was written at a time when Christians were being persecuted by the Roman government. Symbolism and symbolic language were used to convey hope to the Christian churches without putting the members at risk of persecution or death. Numbers had significant meanings to the Jews and early Christians: the number 12 symbolized God's people and perfection; the number 7 also meant perfection; and the number 10 meant power. The woman giving birth symbolizes the Church or Mary.

- In this passage whom do you think the woman represents?
- Why would childbirth be painful for the woman?
- What do you think the dragon represents?
- What happens to the child in this vision?
- What happens to the woman in this vision?
- Who was victorious in this vision?
- What can this vision tell us about God's love and protection?

Taking My Scripture Home

How can you trust God's love and protection in all situations? How can your attitudes and actions reflect that trust?

RESPONSORIAL PSALM REFLECTION: PSALM 45:10bc

- What does it mean to be at someone's *right hand?*
- How can you show utmost respect and awe for Mary?

1 CORINTHIANS 15:20–27

This passage is part of a special section of the first letter to the Corinthians explaining the resurrection of Jesus and those who have died. St. Paul wrote this letter around AD 56.

- What do you suppose *firstfruits* means?
- The Gospel records Jesus raising people from the dead. What was different about Jesus' resurrection?
- Who is the Adam that St. Paul refers to in this passage?
- How did Adam bring death to the world?
- What does it mean to belong to Christ?
- How can you tell if someone belongs to Christ?
- St. Paul writes about how Jesus will reign when he has *put all his enemies under his feet.* Who or what do you suppose is an enemy of Jesus?

Taking My Scripture Home

Do others know that you belong to Christ? Who do you know in your own life that belongs to Christ? What characteristics of this person can you adopt in your life?

LUKE 1:39–56

The Gospel of Luke is the only Gospel to record the story of Mary and Elizabeth. At the time of their encounter, Elizabeth praises Mary for her faith and trust in God. Mary proclaims the mystery of God who works in surprising ways. Elizabeth's child was John the Baptist.

- Why do you think Mary went to see Elizabeth?
- How would you describe the emotions of these two women when they saw each other?
- What did Elizabeth say to Mary?
- Why do you suppose Elizabeth was so humble and respectful to Mary?
- What was Mary's response?
- Whom did Mary praise in her response?
- What do you think this response suggests about the relationship between God and Mary?
- What does this say about Mary's faith and trust in God?

Taking My Scripture Home

Do you proclaim *the greatness of the Lord?* What can you do each day to strengthen your relationship with God and increase your faith and trust in God?

All Saints

November 1

REVELATION 7:2–4, 9–14

The book of Revelation was written at a time when Christians were being persecuted by the Roman government. Symbolism and symbolic language were used to convey hope to the Christian churches without putting the members at risk of persecution or death.

- The author of this letter talks about the *seal of the living God* and of putting that seal *on the foreheads of the servants of our God.* What do you suppose this symbolism means?
- How can you tell if people today are servants of God?
- The author speaks of many people from all nations. What does that tell us about the inclusiveness of the church?
- What does the word *catholic* mean?
- Why do you suppose these multitudes were wearing white?
- What is the mood or atmosphere of this passage?
- Why would this passage be hopeful to us today?

Taking My Scripture Home

How do your attitudes and actions show that you are marked with God's seal? How can you be more inclusive to all those around you?

RESPONSORIAL PSALM REFLECTION: PSALM 24:6

- How do you envision the face of God?
- Why do you long to see God's face?
- Why do you suppose it is important to remember that we are always in the presence of God?

1 JOHN 3:1–3

This letter tries to develop more fully the spiritual life of the community. In this passage the author is contrasting the differences between the ways of the world and the ways of Christians. The author emphasizes that they are, already now, holy and beloved children of God, "saints" in the making.

- How has God bestowed love on people?
- Why do you suppose Christians can be called the children of God?
- What does it mean to be God's children?
- How can you tell by someone's attitudes or actions if he or she is a child of God?
- Why did the author say that the world did not know God?
- How did the world reject Jesus and his teachings?
- How does the world continue to reject Jesus and his teachings today?

Taking My Scripture Home

What are some ways you have experienced God's love in your life? How is God's love revealed to you through the people that love you?

MATTHEW 5:1–12a

This passage was taken from the Sermon on the Mount. At the time Jesus spoke these words, it was commonly believed that wealth was a blessing from God. By contrast it was believed that the poor or sick had done something to provoke God or make God angry. Therefore, the message of the Beatitudes was radical at the time and challenged the people's image of God. The Beatitudes teach us that holiness and happiness go together.

- What type of person or personality do the Beatitudes describe?
- How do you suppose the outcasts of society felt when they heard this sermon?
- Who are the outcasts in today's society?
- How would outcasts be treated if they were looked on by society as blessed?
- In this passage Jesus lists those who are blessed. What does it mean to be *blessed?*
- Why would those listed in this passage be more dependent on God and less dependent on material wealth?
- When are people more dependent on God: when everything is going well or when they are going through a crisis? Explain.

Taking My Scripture Home

When are you more dependent on God? How can you become more dependent on God and less dependent on material things?

SUNDAYS IN THE LITURGICAL YEAR
2006–2030

Year	Lectionary Cycle	First Sunday of Advent	Second Sunday of Ordinary Time	First Sunday of Lent	Easter	Ordinary Time Resumes
2006	B	November 27	January 15	March 5	April 16	June 25 12th Sunday
2007	C	December 3	January 14	February 25	April 8	June 17 11th Sunday
2008	A	December 2	January 20	February 10	March 23	June 1 9th Sunday
2009	B	November 30	January 18	March 1	April 12	June 21 12th Sunday
2010	C	November 29	January 17	February 21	April 4	June 13 11th Sunday
2011	A	November 28	January 16	March 13	April 24	July 3 14th Sunday
2012	B	November 27	January 15	February 26	April 8	June 17 11th Sunday
2013	C	December 2	January 20	February 17	March 31	June 9 10th Sunday
2014	A	December 1	January 19	March 9	April 20	July 6 14th Sunday
2015	B	November 30	January 18	February 22	April 5	June 14 11th Sunday
2016	C	November 29	January 17	February 14	March 27	June 5 10th Sunday
2017	A	November 27	January 15	March 5	April 16	June 25 12th Sunday
2018	B	December 3	January 14	February 18	April 1	June 10 10th Sunday
2019	C	December 2	January 20	March 10	April 21	June 30 13th Sunday
2020	A	December 1	January 19	March 1	April 12	June 21 12th Sunday
2021	B	November 29	January 17	February 21	April 4	June 13 11th Sunday
2022	C	November 28	January 16	March 6	April 17	June 26 13th Sunday
2023	A	November 27	January 15	February 26	April 9	June 18 11th Sunday
2024	B	December 3	January 14	February 18	March 31	June 9 10th Sunday
2025	C	December 1	January 19	March 9	April 20	July 6 14th Sunday
2026	A	November 30	January 18	February 22	April 5	June 14 11th Sunday
2027	B	November 29	January 17	February 14	March 28	June 6 10th Sunday
2028	C	November 28	January 16	March 5	April 16	June 25 12th Sunday
2029	A	December 3	January 14	February 18	April 1	June 10 10th Sunday
2030	B	December 2	January 20	March 10	April 21	June 30 13th Sunday